TEACHER'S MANUAL

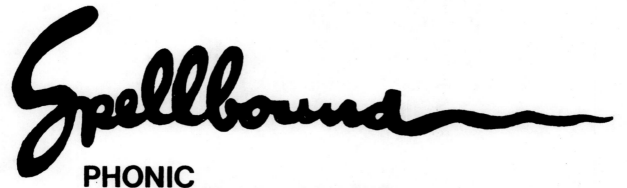

PHONIC
READING & SPELLING

ELSIE T. RAK

Educators Publishing Service, Inc.
Cambridge and Toronto

Educators Publishing Service, Inc.
31 Smith Place, Cambridge, MA   02138

ISBN 0-8388-0166-8

Contents

Introduction 1

Method 1

An Effective Lesson Plan 3

CHAPTER 1 — **The Doubling Rule** 4

CHAPTER 2 — **The Silent E Rule** 7

CHAPTER 3 — **Word Patterns**
F, L, and S; Words like **ALL**; **IGH**;
ILD – OLD words; **Y** as /ī/ at the end of a word;
Y as /ē/ at the end of a word 10

CHAPTER 4 — **Syllable Division and Accent** 16

CHAPTER 5 — **Words You Can Spell**
AR as /är/; **OI** and **OY** as /òi/;
Ways to spell /ò/ (**AU**; **AW**; **AWL** and **AWN**);
OU and **OW** as /aủ/; **OWL** and **OWN**; **OR** as /òr/ 17

CHAPTER 6 — **An Idea Used Four Times**
K and **CK**; **CH** and **TCH**; **GE** and **DGE**;
Words ending in **BLE, DLE**, etc. 27

CHAPTER 7 — **Endings**
NG; **NK**; **LESS** and **NESS**;
FUL and **LY**; **LE** and **LY** 33

CHAPTER 8 — **The Y Rule**
All three Rules 37

CHAPTER 9 — **Vowel Digraphs**
OW as /ō/; **EA** as /ē/; **EA** as /ĕ/;
EA as /ā/; **OO** as /ü/; **OO** as /ủ/;
AI as /ā/; **AY** as /ā/; **EE** as /ē/; **OA** as /ō/ 41

CHAPTER 10 — **Homonyms** 48

CHAPTER 11 — **More Word Patterns**
Words like **PUT** /ủ/; Words like **MOTHER** /ŭ/;
Hard and Soft **C**; Hard and Soft **G**; Words like **YOUNG** /ŭ/;
Silent **K(KN)**; Silent **W(WR)** 48

CHAPTER 12 — **More Endings**
AGE; **WARD**; **TION** /shŭn/; **SION** /zhŭn/; **TURE** 54

CHAPTER 13 — **Word Building** 58

CHAPTER 14 — **Ways to Spell ər**
WOR; **EAR**; **ER**; **IR**; **UR** 59

CHAPTER 15 — **Plurals, Possessives, Contractions** 64

CHAPTER 16 — **The Open Syllable**
Ā; Ē; Ī; Ō; Ū 64

CHAPTER 17 — **Three Lists** 68

CHAPTER 18 — **More Phonograms**
IE as /ē/; **EW**; **EIGH** as /ā/;
UE; Words ending in **EY** 68

CHAPTER 19 — **Problems**
AUGH; **Go**, **Do**; **OUGH**; **ACE**; **ICE**;
ANCE; **AIN** 70

CHAPTER 20 — **More About the Doubling Rule** 72

Introduction

This speller is intended to support a reading program. That spelling does help reading is attested by many high school and college students.

A phonetic approach to reading is of the utmost value in teaching disabled readers. The phonetic system used in conjunction with this speller is the Gillingham set of phonograms.* It is effective. The phonograms are printed in the back of the book but are much more useful on cards.

The dictations are phonetic, except for a few learned words (**was, they**). They have all been used in real situations. This phonetic system is so thorough that the dictations can become elaborate as rapidly as the student can cope with them and still remain phonetic. Many of the more complicated ones were written for students who, two years before, were non-readers.

Don't expect students to understand a rule by reading it themselves. Always explain it. The language used in this speller is as simple as can be written without being reduced to gibberish, so that eventually students should be able to read it. However, some words are uncompromising and cannot be simplified.

The point of view in this manual is that the fundamentals must be taught very rapidly. One reason for this attitude lies in the past history of the students for whom this book is intended. They have failed in reading and writing all of their lives. They must be convinced in the first lesson that they can learn and that the techniques used here are different and effective.

The first thing to do is to establish rapport. You must respect the students. It is important that the students are allowed to show that they are competent in many things. If they make mistakes, assure them that you cannot possibly be shocked, that you have seen every sort of mistake there is. Some students have a well-developed kinesthetic sense and need a scratch pad. It should be available. Students may misspell a word because they originally did not hear it correctly and have mispronounced it for years.

This is a partnership. You can show the students what to do, but they have to do it (not a friend nor a parent). Let each student decide how quickly to proceed through the lessons. Most students are willing to do homework. The students work very hard at this and naturally want to show it to the teacher right away.

If students are inclined to think the phonograms rather simple, they will change their minds as soon as they realize what these phonograms do for their reading and spelling. The phonograms also often help to clarify speech. In one case they eradicated a South Boston accent!

This program can be used with young children also. The principles are the same. Stay longer on the short vowels and the vowel-consonant-e. Put off the long vowel at the end of an open syllable for some time, but do syllable division if appropriate. Cover the phonograms, including the consonants, as soon as possible. A few, such as **y — e** and **y** as/ĭ/, may be omitted. Reading matter is much easier to find for this age.

THE STUDENT MUST HAVE SUCCESS IN WRITING DICTATION AND IN READING IN THE VERY FIRST LESSON.

Method

The Phonograms

The phonograms should be introduced as rapidly as possible and gone over at each lesson until they become automatic. Cram them in. The sooner the students have them all, the better the opportunity is for a decent choice in reading. Most students already know most of the consonant sounds.

Put a phonogram card, for instance **i**, on the desk. The response should be immediate: **i** says /ĭ/ as in **it**, **i** says /ī/ as in **spider**. The letter doesn't "say" anything, but this is a convenient way to express it. Otherwise, many students will omit the sound and say only the key word.

*Anna Gillingham and Bessie W. Stillman, *Phonics Drill Cards for Remedial Reading and Spelling,* (Cambridge, Mass.: Educators Publishing Service, Inc., 1959).

As soon as possible teach the short vowels (**a** says /ă/ as in **apple**), the vowel-consonant-e (**a** says /ā/ as in **safe**), and the long vowel at the end of an open syllable (**a** says /ā/ as in **baby**). The vowel digraphs and diphthongs (**ee, ou, oi, ai,** etc.) should be given as they appear in the reading. Each student will therefore learn the phonograms in a different order and at his or her own personal rate. Always have the students read a list of words containing the new phonogram. When you have introduced more than one way to spell a sound, you will have to tell them, "It is the /ā/ in **sail**."

The Rules

It is highly desirable and almost always possible to plunge right into the heart of the spelling rules. Teach the **doubling rule** in the first lesson, repeating it until the students are temporarily secure. (Three months later you will probably have to do it again.) This rule requires only the short vowels. Follow it by the **silent e rule**, repeating as often as necessary. This rule requires the vowel-consonant-e and eventually the long vowel at the end of an **open syllable**. At the same time, teach **open** and **closed syllables** and syllable division. By the time the **silent e rule** is mastered, the students should be attempting to read the words at the end of **CHAPTER 2, Exercise 6 (tap, tape)** and attempting to read and divide the words at the end of **CHAPTER 4, Exercise 11 (sitting, sited)**. It may take a long time to achieve this. Unless you think the students have been stretched enough and need a rest with something easy from **CHAPTER 3**, go immediately to the **K and CK** generalization in **CHAPTER 6, CH and TCH**, etc.

At this point the students have a very good foundation for both reading and spelling.

Now you can go back to the simpler topics you have by-passed in the earlier chapters. As soon as possible teach the **y** rule. It is an easy rule, but the vocabulary is difficult. During this time the students have been learning phonograms, usually at least one new one in each lesson, often in pairs. Let the students guide you in this.

For many students learning is a spiral. You may want to stop after the ninth or twelfth chapter and start again at the beginning. Don't expect them to remember much the first time around. Learning is also adversely affected by any disturbance, lack of sleep, a bad cold, disharmony in the family, difficulty at school or work. At each repetition you can expect more and include more in the dictation.

It is not necessary to make a commotion over every point. Slip some things in quietly. Whenever there is a "did not" or "was not" in the dictation, dictate as written. After the dictation is read and corrected, show the students how to contract these words. The next time they appear in the dictation, dictate as written and afterward ask the students to do the contraction. By the time you come to a lesson on contractions, the students will have a fair idea of the principle involved. If you use a plural, ask the students what the base word is. Often they can't hear the last sound in the word before the **s**. After they have written it, tell them to add an "**s** — more than one." In this way they will absorb plurals with very little effort. Do the same thing with possessives. If you present pairs of phonograms together (**oi** and **oy**), you can ask which is more likely to be at the end of a word. They will almost know it before you get to the lesson, for by that time the concept is not new.

The Dictation

Most students reading and spelling far below grade level have very poor visual memory. To dictate, you have to rely on auditory discrimination, even if it is weak. This can be done. Gradually the auditory discrimination will improve.

"Dan sat in the grass."

Say the sentence. Have the students repeat it. Then repeat **Dan**. "**Dan**. What is the first sound that you hear?" The students, we hope, say, /d/. If you get /t/, explain voiced and unvoiced letters. "Right. **Dan**. What is the second sound?" "/ă/". "Yes. How do you spell /ă/?" They write the letter **a**. There is often trouble with short vowels, but not usually with /ă/. If necessary, give the key word — **apple**. "Yes. **Dan**. What is the last sound?" /n/. If you get /m/, don't let it pass.

This may seem tedious, but it is fundamental. The students will soon be doing it for themselves without any prompting. If the students don't know how to write a capital letter, give them homework on the alphabet. First have them write a very large letter in the air, then trace it on paper, then copy it. If necessary, prop up the alphabet in front of them.

2

For training in auditory discrimination, dictate nonsense syllables. This will show the students vividly how many attempts they make before they get the correct spelling. It also serves to prove to them that their problem is a disability and not a stupidity.

An Effective Lesson Plan

The Phonograms
Show the cards, one by one. The response, as described, should become automatic.

The Spelling of Sounds
How do you spell the sound /t/?   **t, ed**
How do you spell the sound /ĕ/?   **e, ea**
How do you spell the sound /k/?   **k, c, ck** (ignore **ch**)
How do you spell the sound /ā/?   **a, a-e, ai, ay, ea, eigh, ei, ey**

The student learns these different sounds gradually. The sounds are on the yellow cards in the Gillingham set of phonograms.

The Spelling List
This list is derived from actual misspellings in the dictation or by words representing principles you have taught. Don't put on the list any words involving a principle to be taken up later. Indeed, you should not use such words, but sometimes the students do. Occasionally a learned word may be included. When writing a spelling word, the students should say aloud the name of each letter as they write it.

Review
Review the new work in the previous lesson. With some students this may not be necessary. Many students are so disabled that they can remember very little about language.

Dictation
This presents the new work of the previous lesson.

Reading the Dictation
The students should read the dictation aloud. This is sometimes quite difficult. Many students learn to write better than they can read.

Correcting the Dictation
The students should be able to correct their errors themselves. If they cannot, then you know they are confused and the appropriate concept must be reviewed.

New Work or Review

A Variety of Topics
Many items must eventually be covered: **open** and **closed syllables**, syllable division, accent, blending, long vowel at the end of an **open syllable, nk** and **ng**, hard and soft **c** and **g**, nonsense syllables, word building, word games, comprehension exercises, etc.

Reading Aloud
Reading matter for these older people who are reading far below grade level is very difficult to find. Use your public library. Librarians are interested in your problem and know books. They can often suggest exactly the right one.

Do not give poor readers simple books in the area of their individual competence, even if you think they should be interested in the vocabulary. The person who guards a missile site does not care to read a third grade book on missiles. In general avoid science fiction. The vocabulary is usually large and sometimes invented and many of the effects are made by implication. These students have enough trouble with flat statements. You may find exceptions both in books and in students. Completely phonetic stories may be useful, but should not be used extensively, since they do not represent what the students will meet in real life.

The Doubling Rule

CHAPTER 1

Exercise 1 — page 3

reddish	biggest	sipping	snapping
redness	fatness	dragging	gladden
dropping	fattest	witness	gladness

Exercise 2 — pages 5 and 6

flatter	hotter	gripping	ripped
flatly	slipper	rusty	planning
singing	rested	hidden	risky
hotly	witty	blotter	

Exercise 3 — page 6

er	ly	ed	ing	y	en

Exercise 4 — pages 6 and 7

gunner	quitting*	crispy	scrapping
jammed	flipped	mapped	funny
helper	faster	sunny	wetness
pinning	grinned	dimmer	shutters
dusty	slimmer	dimly	

Exercise 5 — page 8

badly	bandage	robber	fibber
brighten	buzzer	meeting	farming
sparked	tramped	illness	chipped
goodness	starry	beggar	colder
luggage			

Exercise 6 — pages 9 and 10

stacked	banker	strictly	floppy
tubby	fretting	boldest	pointed
bookish	fretful	stepping	lobby
warring	pounded	swifter	hitter
bitter	shredded	scarring	milked
garbage	steamer	stabbed	pennant
cribbage	bidders	failing	harder
wooden			

*Point out that **qu** is a unit, therefore there is only one vowel in this word. It is one, one, one.

Exercise 7 — page 11

ed   y   ish   ing   er   age   en   ful   ly   est   ant

Dictation 1

The puppy gripped the slipper. Dan hunted for it madly. It was hidden under the bed.

Dictation 2

Sal was running to get the bus. She slipped and landed in the gutter, ripping her pants.

Dictation 3

Pam slipped and fell on the grass. Her puppy came up and smelled her and barked. Pam patted the pup and got up.

Dictation 4

Tom found a plum and ate it. It was bitter and made him shudder. He flipped the pit up and got a drink from the pond. His hands were dripping wet.

Dictation 5

Tom was planning to drive. It was slippery and he started skidding. The car slipped to the side, but he stopped in time.

Dictation 6

Pat dropped the glass. It shattered. She slipped on bits of glass and skidded on the path but she stopped in time.

Dictation 7

Mark planned to take a sun bath. He flopped onto the grass in a sunny spot. The puppy came running up and tripped over him and started licking him. Mark grimly gave up.

Dictation 8

We were hunting for the hidden book. We flipped over the lids of cans, tapped boxes and tripped all over ourselves.

Dictation 9

The pond was choppy. The wind was whipping the branches of the trees. The sun was hidden. A flag was flapping madly. Jan slipped inside.

Dictation 10

The road was dimly lit. The colder and darker it got, the faster I drove. I just wanted to get home.

Dictation 11

Liz looked grimly at the heater. It was pounding and getting hotter. Stopping it was risky, for it was getting colder outside.

Dictation 12

Dan dropped his key. It skidded on the grass and slipped into the gutter and got hidden under the trash.

Dictation 13

It was a foggy day and very muggy. Fran slipped down to the pond and went swimming. Getting out, she stubbed her toe on a rock and yelled madly. She was hotter than ever.

Dictation 14

I stuffed the trash into the car and slipped off to the dump. The day was sunny and getting brighter and hotter. I planned on going swimming.

Dictation 15

Don chopped the weeds and quickly scrubbed the driveway. Then he jumped into the car, snapped on the lights, and clipped along to Peg's house.

Dictation 16

The pond was hidden by the trees. Pat was tripping along when she saw it. Her puppy started running to it, barking at the fish and lapping up a drink. Pat got a stone and skipped it.

Dictation 17

I found the pin. It was hidden in the copper box. I planned to put it on for the party.

Dictation 18

The tramp was sloppy. He had baggy pants and lacked a scrubbing. He slipped into a hidden ditch and napped.

Dictation 19

The batter stepped into the box. He was hitting well and getting better. He slammed the ball into the stands. As he started running, the fans clapped and yelled.

Dictation 20

The kittens were scrapping madly in the yard. They slipped all over the muddy grass. I put milk out for them, and they came running.

Dictation 21

At the meeting he put the buzzer in his luggage so it was hidden.

Dictation 22

Jan stepped off the platform. She started getting onto solid ground but her foot got stuck beside the platform in motion. She slipped and fell and dislocated her knee cap.

Dictation 23

Tom dragged out his cutter and trimmed the hedge. He scrubbed the driveway. After chopping some wood, he slipped down to Mark's cottage to play cribbage.

Dictation 24

Sam slipped on the hill and started to fall over the cliff. He grabbed a shrub and stopped his fall. Finding a hidden hole, he jammed his foot into it. He shuddered and hoped he was not trapped. The hill was very rugged.

Dictation 25

Val gripped the key. Stepping onto the porch, she jammed the key into the lock. She slapped at it and hammered it madly. She was getting hotter and hotter and madder and madder. Then she gave up, tripped on the step, and slipped off in a temper to her car.

Dictation 26

Bill clipped the grass and milked the cow. Gripping the bucket, he went into the barn. The bucket slipped and the milk flipped all over. Bill was the maddest man you ever saw.

Dictation 27

Meg tripped on the path and slipped and fell. She ripped her pants and skinned her arm. She gritted her teeth and did not cry. She jumped up and planned to go home. She scrubbed her arm and changed her pants.

Dictation 28

The child saw the plate of cakes, dripping with icing. He stepped up and took the biggest cake and started stuffing it. It flipped over in his hand and dropped with a splash. The icing was all over him and he had to be scrubbed.

Dictation 29

It is not fitting to have a snowstorm on Easter Sunday. It was very slippery. Cars skidded and stalled.

Dictation 30

I skimmed over the dusty road in my tubby little car and skidded to a stop at the top of the hill. There I saw the sea. The waves were lapping at the shore, the sky was sunny and the long grass was flapping in the wind. Then I dropped down to the sand.

Dictation 31

The dog was trapped in the dripping hole and was barking madly. Beth started running to see what was the matter. The sides of the hole were so steep and high that the dog was helpless. Beth dragged a plank over and slipped it into the hole. She gripped it and the dog stepped up. He was so happy that he slobbered all over Beth. Beth was happy too.

Dictation 32

I was a witness to the crash. The truck slipped on the ice and clipped the little car. This man jumped out and gave the truck driver a helping hand.

Dictation 33

The weather was rugged, but the Christmas lights shimmered in the dusk. Jen shrugged into her coat, wrapped herself against the bitter cold and went out into the street, trimmed with lights and jammed with shoppers.

Dictation 34

It was a sunny day but the wind was getting stronger. Tom walked briskly down to the sandy beach. The waves were choppy, the flag on the Coast Guard Station was flapping madly, the stubby beach grass was snapping in the breeze and the surf was slapping and pounding on the rocky shore. Tom, gripping his fishing rod, found the hidden cove, but the wind was driving in too swiftly for casting. He dropped down on the sand and planned on resting until the wind lifted.

Dictation 35

Jim was bragging about his skill in the game of chess. Dripping scorn on the players, he patted himself on the back. Then Jan sailed into him, nabbed him, and gave him a drubbing.

The Silent E Rule

CHAPTER 2

Exercise 1 — pages 15 and 16

safety	careless	likable	nameless
used	famous	tiresome	wisely
using	wading	grateful	likeness
stony	soreness	driver	

Exercise 2 — page 16

ing   ful   ty   ed   y   less   ous   ness   able   some   er   ly

Exercise 3 — pages 16 and 17

smoky	icy	likeness	poker
smokeless	homeless	riding	sizable
notable	lazy	spicy	

Exercise 4 — pages 17 and 18

tuneful	taking	lonesome	ripeness
spineless	spiteful	shady	placing
biting	priceless	joker	displacement
rated	flaming	shiny	

Exercise 5 — pages 18 and 19

advisable	blamed	wasteful	shameless
amazement	distasteful	gravely	invitation
debatable	quotation	gravity	combination
blameless	educator	hateful	

Dictation 1

The sun was shining on the pond. Tom sat in a shady spot. The wind was waving the grass.

Dictation 2

The driving rain made the path slippery. Dale skidded, but she got home safely.

Dictation 3

Taking his rod, Sam slipped along the stony path to the pond. Hoping to get a fish, he cast his line. He snagged a big fish.

Dictation 4

Kate was hoping to go on a trip. She planned on taking a useful bag. After cramming in a lot of things, she dropped it into the car and started driving.

Dictation 5

In the blazing sun a number of cows were grazing gravely on the grass. They were thriving.

Dictation 6

The car next to Sam started skidding. He was hopeful of sliding to the side without hitting it. He braked carefully and avoided a flaming crash.

Dictation 7

Jane was driving her shiny new car up the icy hill. The night was dark and stormy. The wind was waving branches and hitting the car.

Dictation 8

June went down the shady path to the shining pond. She was hoping to see some tadpoles. She saw some swimming at the edge. She waded into the pond, and happily watched them play.

Dictation 9

The man was a careless driver, taking a lot of room on the road. He speeded up and almost caused a fatal crash.

Dictation 10

Bob was driving down the hill, looking at the flaming sunset. He was hoping to get home by dark.

Dictation 11

Sal liked the noisy puppy, even when it whined shamelessly for more bones. Sal cared for her puppy lovingly.

Dictation 12

The winter day was icy. The snow at the side of the road was black. It was tiresome to deliver goods in the noisy truck. Then the truck shook very hard and broke down.

Dictation 13

With a careful finger Roy was stroking the noisy snapping puppy, hoping to see his tag. He was a stray dog and was probably missed by some child.

Dictation 14

Kate was riding her shiny new bike down the driveway, hopeful of getting to school on time. A dog came out of the woods and barked at her. She tipped over, scraping the bike and ripping her pants. She was scared.

Dictation 15

Pam was hoping the day might stay bright. She was going down the stony path when she took a careless step and twisted her ankle. She did not want to use it. Wisely she sat down and skidded the rest of the way. It was not graceful, but she got home.

Dictation 16

Franco was going slowly, taking his time. The sunset was flaming, the lake was shining with light, and the hay was waving in the wind. He wisely stopped to look.

Dictation 17

They were playing poker in a disgracefully smoky room. It was amazing that they did not feel it. They were extremely intent on the cards and did not think of griping.

Dictation 18

Jim was griping about the heat. It was getting hazy. Then he stepped down to the pond and went diving and swimming. When he got out he lay down in a shady spot.

Dictation 19

Kim was driving down the street. The car ahead of her stopped very quickly. Kim couldn't stop safely in time and bumped into it.

Dictation 20

The sun was shining brightly. Jim was getting on his bike. He was planning on riding to the park.

Dictation 21

Tom was driving madly down the icy road, hoping to get to the job on time. His tires were whining and he skidded. He stopped the car safely, but was hazy about how he did it.

Dictation 22

Rose was driving her car down a lonesome, shady lane. It was both rutted and stony, so she drove carefully. The graceful branches of the trees were waving in the wind, showing sunny spots. The birds were noisy. A small snake glided across the path. The air was spicy. Rose was famous for driving fast, but now she was entirely happy to be slipping quietly along.

Dictation 23

Fran was hoping to reach home before the storm. The wind was extremely strong and very noisy, whipping the trees around. It had a lonesome sound. The rain came with spiteful strength. Fran skidded a little and wisely slowed down the car. In the hazy air it would not do to be careless.

Dictation 24

Mark plodded down the lonely road in the flaming heat. Striding to the side he found a shady spot and dropped down carelessly to rest. There was a sound. Looking around hopefully, he saw a noisy brook. He smiled and drank the icy water.

Dictation 25

A shiny red diner is a useful thing. You can come in from the bitter cold and sniff the enticing air. It may be noisy, but the activity is inviting. You are not likely to be lonesome. You can safely put the car in the driveway and eat a sizable meal.

Dictation 26

I was hopeful of having an admirable day. However, it was notable for its tiresome blunders. Nothing went right. I wisely went home and got gratefully into bed.

Dictation 27

Hope was hopelessly wakeful. Finally she shrugged fatefully and slipped noiselessly out of bed. Putting on some old clothes, she stepped outside into the intensely bitter cold. Sliding on the icy driveway, she got to the street and went groping along for a mile. She found the biting cold a stimulating sensation. Then she went back on the dimly lighted street. When she got home, she was grateful for a warm bed.

Word Patterns

CHAPTER 3

F, L and S

Dictation 1

Tell Ms. Muffet her dress is a mess.
The bell is ringing for class.
Can we drill for a well?
Get a whiff of that smell.
The boy fell off the cliff.
Pat is a big bluff.

Dictation 2

Pam got a whiff of the cut grass. It smelled grand. She fell and got her dress mussed.

Dictation 3

The car puffed up the hill.

Dictation 4

Sam was getting a pill. He hit his hand on the sink and the glass spilled. After he wiped up the mess, he was so late he missed the train.

Dictation 5

It was dull in the house. Dan slipped out to the sand. Gulls were skimming the waves, getting fish in the swells. It was blissful to smell the sharp air.

Dictation 6

Jill felt cross. It was a dull morning. She sniffed the smell from the passing cars. The wind tossed the dust in her nose. Life was a mess.

Dictation 7

Bill sniffed the smell of the waves. The grass was waving in the wind. A ship was making puffs of smoke.

Dictation 8

Standing on a cliff, Bess looked at the swells and sniffed the sharp smell. Waves were tossing things on the sand and the gulls were getting fish with skill.

Dictation 9

It was a dull day. A mass of clouds hid the sun. Jan packed without fuss. She was not pressed for time and had the morning to kill because the plane was late.

Dictation 10

The dog tossed his head and barked at the pile of wood. A porcupine ambled out from under it and crossed the grass. The dog started sniffing it and the creature shot some quills. The dog crossed over the pile of wood and just barely escaped.

Words like ALL

Dictation 1

Do not call to the cat. She will jump off the wall and start slipping in the tall wet grass.

Dictation 2

Jill was running in the hall with a ball in her hand. She started to fall and hit the wall. The ball fell and rolled down the hall. She sobbed.

Dictation 3

It is a tall order, but I hope the team can win the baseball game. They have fallen down on the job. They keep stalling.

Dictation 4

The wall was rather tall. Jim slipped off it and dropped. His fall was hard. He hit a hidden stone and banged his leg. He had to call for help.

Dictation 5

Val was fishing from her pram. The sun began to fall. She saw a squall line coming on like a dark wall. By luck the wind pushed the pram ashore.

Dictation 6

Bob went down the hall, calling to his dog. The dog saw him but stalled. Bob called and called, but the dog went off with his ball.

Dictation 7

The tall man filled the hall and made it look small. He came to call on his boss. He was ill. The tall man took him a book.

Dictation 8

It was a very hot day. There came a sudden squall with strong winds and heavy rain. The children ran joyfully out into it and had a ball.

Dictation 9

The squall made a wall of snow falling in front of the car. Jess had to drive so slowly that she almost stalled.

Dictation 10

Tom hit the ball off the wall and broke the glass pane. He did not want to tell his mother and stalled for time. Then he got a call to go inside. Tom's mother made him fix it and gave him a better ball. He did not need a better ball. He needed to be a better batter.

IGH

Dictation 1

The sight of the men fighting on the cliff frightened Fran. She sighed. A slight slip might make them fall.

Dictation 2

April saw the flight of the plane high in the sky. It was a grand sight. She might try flying herself.

Dictation 3

Last night I went to a show. There was some fighting in it that made a frightful noise. It was quite a sight. I went home quite upset.

Dictation 4

The night was fine and the sky was filled with stars. Right after dinner Mark's flight took off. From the plane the lighted city was a splendid sight.

Dictation 5

It was a bright day. Frank saw the flight of a plane. It was a grand sight. When it started dropping, it gave him a fright. No, it was all right.

Dictation 6

Ed was mad and hit Tom with all his might. Tom fell. He was madder than Ed. He got up fast and blasted Ed. It was a grand fight and might have lasted all night. After that Ed and Tom became pals.

Dictation 7

The moon was high and the night was delightful. Then Bob saw a frightening sight. A person was slinking into the barn. Bob sat tight.

Dictation 8

At night the bright lights of the city could be seen for miles. What a sight. When they suddenly went out, it was frightening.

Dictation 9

The night sky was filled with the light of the stars. It was almost as bright as day. However, it was frightfully cold. I went right back in.

Dictation 10

The child was frightened by the thunder and lightning. At night it was very bright. With a sigh, she ran into the lighted kitchen, where she felt safe.

Dictation 11

Peg went out into the bright morning with her dog. She saw a bird. She gripped the dog tightly but the pup made a slight noise. The bird was frightened and took flight.

Dictation 12

Jane was going down the street at night. A car turned in and the bright lights blinded her. It barely missed her and took off in flight. It was such a tight corner that she was frightened.

Dictation 13

It was night and in the dim light Kate saw a dark shape. She did not let it frighten her. She snapped on the lamp. It was a big cat.

Dictation 14

High on the cliff the two men were standing in the bright moonlight. The girl could see Fred on the edge of the cliff. It was quite frightening. The flight of an owl split them apart. Fred got out of that tight spot.

Dictation 15

A light rain fell in the night, making the world bright and shiny. At high noon the sun came out. A tight little cluster of people gathered to see the boats in the public garden. Spring was slightly sensational.

Dictation 16

It was a wild night. High in the sky the bolts of lightning flashed boldly. It was quite a sight. Sam and his date were badly frightened and clung.

ILD-OLD Words

Dictation 1

The colt was wild and did not mind Jill. Jill scolded him and told him to behave.

Dictation 2

The mold on the grinder had a blinding smell. It must have been old or the freezer must not have been cold.

Dictation 3

I had a jolt and my box is slipping. Kindly get hold of it before I fold up.

Dictation 4

The colt bolted with the child. It was a wild ride, but he did not mind. He held on and boldly enjoyed it.

Dictation 5

I stole the gold and boldly ran to my car. I had a wild ride, going blindly in the snow.

Dictation 6

The wild colt bolted with the child. That jolted June with fright. She started running and boldly grabbed the strap. The child fell off and started grinning with the fun of it.

Dictation 7

The sheep was blindly stuck in the long grass in the pond. Tom boldly went in and took hold of it and led it ashore. It was kind of him, for it was very cold.

Dictation 8

Bess rounded a blind corner and felt a jolt. The old car started to grind to a stop and simply folded up. What a wild thing to have happen. She could find nothing the matter.

Dictation 9

The day was wild. It was cold and raw. The snow was blinding. Behind the bold line of cloud was a queer gold light.

Dictation 10

The child got lost in the snowdrifts. She was finding it very slippery. Holding on to a post, she saw the way home. When she got to the house, tired and cold, her mother did not scold her but told her to take off her wet things.

Dictation 11

Mary scolded herself, for she kept thinking of the test. She could not keep her mind off it. She felt as wild as a colt. She told herself that she should not be behind the others and made herself go boldly in.

Dictation 12

Did that child find the old gold ring? It is kind that the child did not mind and told the person on patrol.

Dictation 13

The cold was biting. The wind blew wildly from the snowy hills. Mark, following the trail blindly, did not know how long he could hold out. Behind him were unbroken miles of hiking. Well, he would keep his mind on his goal and grind out the rest of the way, step by step.

Y as /ī/ at the end of a word

Dictation 1

Hope has a cat. The cat is hot. It sits in the shade. Why not? The grass is dry.

Dictation 2

A car was passing by. A plane was flying in the sky. A dog was running by the yard. Why not try the new bike?

Dictation 3

I am spying on my child. Why is she crying? I will dry her cheeks and give her a glass of milk.

Dictation 4

Get dry sticks. Make a fire. Fry the ham.

Dictation 5

Why do you spy on me, you sly thing? Why do you try to pry into my home? Stop crying and dry your cheeks. Now go away.

Dictation 6

The spry old person went up and down the streets, trying to spy on the children. Why was this person so sly?

Dictation 7

The spy was trying to pry into things. He poked around. Kim was shy but she got smart and stopped the spy cold.

Dictation 8

Jim called to the crying child. She did not reply. He told her to dry her cheeks. Shyly she did try and began to smile.

Dictation 9

Why not try to fish? Dan dropped a fly on the pond. It was a good day for the sky was gray. He got his fish and made a fire to fry it.

Dictation 10

As I was frying chops, I was called to the phone. The dog tried to take them on the sly and got hot. My how he did fly.

Dictation 11

The spy snatched the secret papers and started running. The spry old person cried out. The spy tried to fly off but the cop stopped her.

Dictation 12

How to fry a fish.

First you have to catch it. Why not cut a hole in the ice on a pond? Tie your line to two sticks that are crossed. Go home to a good fire. When the fish takes the hook, a lever with a red flag will pop us. When you see that, go out of the warm room, get the fish, clean and scale it, wipe it dry and fry it in butter. Eat it.

Dictation 13

Try as he might, Fred could not fry an egg. It was always dry. He could hardly pry it out of the pan and was ready to cry with frustration.

Dictation 14

The spy was prying into the desk. She was a sly spy, but not very smart. By bumping into the desk, she dropped her bag with a thud. Tom saw her, gave a cry, and sent her flying.

Y as /ē/ at the end of a word

Dictation 1

Carry the empty glass to the man. He will get the milk and fill it.

Dictation 2

I drove fifty dusty miles. I stopped for gas and got a can of coke.

Dictation 3

It was a windy day. The child was chilly. Bob started to get him candy but the box was empty.

Dictation 4

It was a funny kind of a day. The wind had a nasty sting. The air was damp and chilly. Betty got some logs and made a fire.

Dictation 5

It is silly to start out with so little gas. Soon the tank will be empty. Then you will have a nasty, chilly hike to the next pump.

Dictation 6

The empty house was spooky and chilly. Peggy went out into the windy night. She was fifty or sixty miles away and she had a flat tire.

Dictation 7

The jelly jar is empty. It is a funny thing, but it always seems to be empty. Maybe the thing is that Henry is a bully and is forever grabbing it. He is a nasty boy.

Dictation 8

Betsy was so thrifty that she pinched pennies. She was happy to save on anything, even jelly. She got to be not so much silly as nasty.

Dictation 9

Henry was always happy to save a penny. He was very thrifty. He got an old Honda for twenty-five, fixed it up, and made fifty when he sold it.

Dictation 10

Roy was going to fish. The wide sand was empty because the gray morning was windy and chilly. The tide was running in. He got twenty-six fish.

Dictation 11

It was chilly and windy by the pond. Sid did not mind. She likes to fish and had her rod. She cast her line and got a fighting fish. She got twenty-six fish.

Dictation 12

Dick was stopped by the train. He counted sixty empty flatcars. They rattled by on the dusty tracks.

Dictation 13

Mark got bread and jelly and went outside. It was so windy that the food fell out of his hand. It got sandy and rather messy, but he did not mind. Being thrifty, he ate it.

Dictation 14

It was a nasty, chilly day in spring. The yard was messy. The grass was filthy with winter rubbish. Then the sun came out and made us happy. Isn't it funny how silly we are?

Dictation 15

Sam opened the package and began to eat the candy. Sitting on the porch, he looked at the empty landscape simmering in the sunny air. It was silly to be so happy doing nothing.

Dictation 16

The child dropped her candy on the dusty ground. It was filthy. Being thrifty, she picked up the nasty thing and stuck it in her mouth. Tommy yelled at her, "I have told you fifty times not to do that." The child just grinned.

Syllable Division and Accent

CHAPTER 4

Exercises 1 and 2 — pages 28 and 29

fún	ny		tún	nel		pút	ty
bét	ter		bót	tle		kén	nel
táf	fy		com	mánd		múf	fin
at	témpt		shát	ter		sup	póse

Exercises 3 and 4 — page 29

criḿ	son		wín	dow		eń	ter
un	tíl		in	váde		for	bíd
uń	der		for	gét		táb	let
más	ter		ch́im	ney			

Exercise 5 — page 30

bō	open		sē	open		ĕb	closed
ăp	closed		ĭd	closed		cū	open
tī	open		mō	open		dē	open
ŏb	closed		dū	open		ŏm	closed
rē	open		ĕp	closed		rō	open
mū	open		ăg	closed		ŭg	closed
ăd	closed		kē	open		ĭc	closed
ĭp	closed		sī	open		pī	open
fā	open		tā	open		ŭd	closed
ŏt	closed		ŏc	closed		ăc	closed
			pō	open		lā	open
			ŭf	closed		ĕt	closed

Exercise 6 — page 31

brī	open		cŭm	closed		frī	open
ŭll	closed		prē	open		ŏnt	closed
prō	open		drī	open		ĕsk	closed
ĭst	closed		ŭsk	closed		scā	open
shā	open		sprī	open		ŭsp	closed
plō	open		ĭft	closed		grū	open
ŭsh	closed		ŭpt	closed		trō	open
dĭs	closed		trā	open		ĭlt	closed
spū	open		ŏmp	closed		ămp	closed
ăst	closed		glō	open		brē	open
twī	open		plū	open		ŭft	closed
clō	open		ŏct	closed		spō	open

trăns	closed		ĕlt	closed		strū	open
cŏn	closed		splē	open		ŏst	closed
			ŭlk	closed		scrī	open
			scŏ	open		ĕlp	closed

Exercises 8 and 9 — page 33

próp	er		rú	mor		tráv	el
chó	sen		stú	pid		lá	bel
bó	nus		plán	et		ú	nit
wíd	ow		hú	man		sí	ren
vé	to		pú	pil			

Words You Can Spell

The words at the end of these word lists are usually more difficult or more sophisticated. You may want to omit some of them at first.

The students may confuse **au** and /ŏ/ and in New England, **or**. You may want to postpone **au** and **aw**. You may want to omit **owl, own, awl** and **awn** the first time around. **Bound, ground,** etc., appear to be difficult and may require a separate lesson.

AR as /är/

Dictation 1

Carl marched to the farm and got a jar of jam. It was not far.

Dictation 2

Mark parked the car in the tarred driveway. A large dog barked at him and jumped at the car. Mark got out of the yard fast.

Dictation 3

Nan drives into the yard and parks the car by the barn. It is a fine night with stars in the sky.

Dictation 4

A spark from lightning started a fire in the hay in the barn. Ann started the pump by the pond and stopped the fire.

Dictation 5

When Mark came home he was always starved. He slipped in the marble hall and jarred his arm. It did no real harm. Then he went into the kitchen and ate an apple tart.

Dictation 6

The artist made a sketch of the charming old barn. She was startled to see that part of it was pink. They were harvesting apples and packing them for the market. She felt so starved that she barged in and asked for some.

Dictation 7

Jane went to the market. There was quite a snarl of cars in the parking lot. She got tart apples and sharp cheese. That makes a fine combination.

Dictation 8

Ted was starving when he came home. All he could find was a sparkling jar of pickles. He started eating them, thinking there would be no harm in that. He was mistaken. He was startled by a sharp pain, which took the charm out of it.

Dictation 9

Down by the barn the dog was snarling. I was startled. I darted down to see what was the matter. I hoped that it was not a skunk that sparked that barking. No, it was a harmless snake.

Dictation 10

Mark was starving. He started to pass a market garden where they were selling large red apples and stopped to get just one. The artist in charge sold him a basket of them.

Dictation 11

Val gave a party in the barn. She strung up some sparkling lights and hung up artists' posters. She put a dart board at the end and filled an old farm cart with red apples. It was charming.

Dictation 12

The child got in the parked car and let the brake go. The car started running down the hill. Dogs barked at it. It made a sharp turn, snarling up traffic. It stopped in the yard of a startled shopkeeper.

Dictation 13

Mr. Smith had a lot of apple trees. When the apples were harvested he put a cart full of them at one corner of the crossroads and put his son in charge of selling them. Cars stopped. Many were charmed to find them tart, sharp and crisp. They went like hotcakes.

Dictation 14

Frank drained the crankcase and put in new spark plugs. He charged the man for parts and labor. The man did not pay cash but used his credit card.

Dictation 15

Pam made a scarf with red yarn. It wasn't hard. She was startled to see how charming she looked. She felt like a real artist.

Dictation 16

The march caused a snarl of cars on its way to the park. It started with a brass band in scarlet. They were sharp and the songs were charming. The horns sparkled in the sun.

Dictation 17

The farmer charted his way down the barnyard in the darkness. Suddenly he was startled by a rattling sound. He tripped over an old cart and jarred his arm, but it was not harmed. Then he saw two sparkling yellow spots. It was the darned cat.

Dictation 18

It was as dark as tar. Even the stars were hidden. The dog was barking sharply. When he started to snarl, Dale went to the barn. A spark had set an old ladder on fire. She filled a bucket and got it out. Good old dog!

OI as /ȯi/

Dictation 1

Do not get the joint moist. I am oiling it. Do not spoil the job.

Dictation 2

Jane was trying to fish. A noisy bunch of boys came to the lake to swim and spoiled her sport. It made her boiling mad.

Dictation 3

Dave went into the joint to avoid the storm. It was very noisy. The air smelled of spoiling food. He went right out again. It was better to get wet.

Dictation 4

Do not boil the coffee. That will spoil it.

Dictation 5

Don stuck a coin in the slot and joined Sandy in a cup of coke. Sandy stuck one in another slot and played a noisy song.

Dictation 6

It was foggy, so the air was moist and the noises were muffled. It did not spoil the day for Liz. She liked fog.

Dictation 7

Sam joined the boys in a noisy game of baseball. The point was to have fun. His dog got in the way with his joyful barking and almost spoiled the game.

Dictation 8

Eve was spading the moist soil. She saw a snake coiled to spring so she grabbed her hoe. The dog barked noisily but the snake was harmless. Eve went back to destroying the weeds.

Dictation 9

Pam turned on the coffee. The joint of the chest in the kitchen was noisy so she oiled it. This took time and the coffee boiled over.

Dictation 10

The snake was coiled to strike and rattling noisily. Dale tried to hit it with a rock, but her aim was spoiled. She joined the others in flight.

Dictation 11

In avoiding the child, Tom had no choice but to turn the car to the left. A puppy dashed out and spoiled his aim. He crashed into a tree. At this point he was boiling mad.

Dictation 12

Spring was in the air. The river was very noisy. In the moist woods the moss grew green on the rock slabs, wherever there was a little soil. The birds joined in song, rejoicing over the crisp, bright air.

Dictation 13

Bill had some soiled things to take to the laundromat. He stuck a coin in the slot but forgot to shut the clamp. In a noisy rush the mess slopped together on the ground. Bill became a trifle moist and more than a trifle red.

Dictation 14

Mary was hiking up to the top. She had to hoist herself over a steep cliff. Too late she saw that poison ivy was growing all over it. She could not avoid it, but she would not let it spoil her fun. Soon she came to a noisy stream with moist branches. She had a very refreshing drink.

OY as /ȯi/

Dictation 1

The boy was employed in destroying the poison ivy. He enjoyed it.

Dictation 2

It was a joyful day under a bright sky. Pat was employed in raking the garden and found it very enjoyable.

Dictation 3

The child was annoyed and slammed his toy on the ground. It is a good thing it was not his father's best dish that he destroyed.

Dictation 4

It was a joyful day. Anne was happily employed in the kitchen, baking cookies. Not even a storm could destroy the fun.

Dictation 5

Ben was playing with his toy poodle, employed in scratching him on the back. The puppy enjoyed it very much.

Dictation 6

The puppy enjoyed destroying the baby's ball. It employed every trick with joyful barks. Joy was annoyed and got the little boy another ball. The puppy destroyed that toy also.

Dictation 7

The shutter was noisy, so Roy oiled the joints. While he was thus employed, his dog was digging up the soil, destroying the garden and spoiling the plants. Roy got boiling mad.

Dictation 8

Kit was employed in her garden, destroying weeds. A child was playing with a toy poodle. Kit saw the boy enjoying his noisy game and smiled.

Dictation 9

Ted recalled his boyhood and how he enjoyed playing handball. He tried it again and was annoyed to find that he had lost his skill. It destroyed the fun. He toyed with the idea of getting a yo-yo.

Dictation 10

Jan enjoyed the snow, for she liked to ski. It annoyed Roy. His bike slipped and skidded on the road. He was employed in avoiding a crash.

AU as /ȯ/

Dictation 1

Ann haunted the shop because she had to get fresh lumber.

Dictation 2

Paul paused at the gate because he liked to look at the yard. Then he hauled the hose to the garden.

Dictation 3

I needed to haul my stuff to the laundromat. Outside, I paused. It was a bright and gusty August day.

Dictation 4

In August Paul haunted the garden. He hauled in peat because it makes the plants grow. After that, he had to launder his pants.

Dictation 5

Paul made a jaunt to the dump, hauling his trash. It was fun, because he took potshots at the cans.

Dictation 6

Roy hauled off on a jaunt into the hills because of the haunting red and yellow trees.

Dictation 7

A fault lay below the volcano, causing it to erupt in August. Eve made a jaunt out to see it. It was a frightening sight.

Dictation 8

It was a bright and shining day in August. Mary was hauling trash to the dump and was late. She paused to feel the breeze. Was it her fault the day was so grand?

Dictation 9

Pat had a lot of laundry. It was not her fault. When Paul played in the yard with the puppy, he got very messy. She hauled it to the laundromat, stuck in some coins, and got it all clean.

Dictation 10

Dan went to the laundromat. He stuck some coins in the slot and water splashed all over. No one found the cause, but it was not his fault. That is no way to run a laundry.

Dictation 11

They tried to haul the trash to the dump, but it was closed. Jane said it was her fault because she had not paused to look at the announcement of the time when it was open.

Dictation 12

Holding his cup and saucer and sipping his coffee, Dan paused at the window. The garden was quite dry because of the August heat. He formed the notion of turning on the faucet and running the hose over it.

Dictation 13

Pam had a car crash. It was not her fault, but it haunted her because she had hit a dog. She was hauling wood and paused at the stop light. A car on the left turned in widely and hit her and made her car go into the dog.

Dictation 14

Tom made a jaunt to the haunted house. He paused by the gate. He jammed his hand in it and cut it. It was raw.

AW as /ȯ/

Dictation 1

Sandy will draw a map on the sand with a straw.

Dictation 2

It is unlawful to hit a cop on the jaw.

Dictation 3

The outlaw started to draw his gun. He was going to shoot the squaw. The gun jammed and he had to run from the law.

Dictation 4

The outlaw pawed in the straw to hide the gold. Then, drawing his gun and clamping his jaw, he hid in the back of the barn and waited for the law. If the cops came, he would give them a raw deal.

Dictation 5

The outlaw clawed her way over the drifts of snow. In spite of the raw wind, it was thawing. She tried to hurry but slipped and skidded. She wanted to get the cash hidden before the law could catch her.

Dictation 6

The cat clawed in the straw, looking for food. A bird squawked, trying to draw him away from her nest.

Dictation 7

Ann was driving along, a car crashed into her. She bumped her arm, but she didn't care a straw for that. Her dog got her paw smashed. Ann was going to get a lawyer for that. The driver should be outlawed.

Dictation 8

The child patted the cat. The cat flicked its paw at the child's jaw and made raw red lines with its claws. Dawn laid down the law and put the cat out of the house.

Dictation 9

The dog clawed the house, hoping to get in, and left a raw spot on the wall. There was no use talking to the law, so Mark got out the paint and fixed it.

Dictation 10

It was a raw day in March. The wind was blowing lawlessly. The dirty snow was thawing recklessly onto the roads, only to freeze at night, making the driving slippery. The straw sprawled limply on the rose beds. Who says we don't have spring in New England?

Dictation 11

The outlaw was using rather raw language. James clamped his jaw to keep his temper. Then his mood began to thaw. After all, an outlaw needs a lawyer more than anyone.

Dictation 12

The man tapped raw weed into his pipe. He clamped his jaw onto it, lit it, and made it draw. If you like the smell, it is good. If you do not, it is a stench. The room was so smoky that you had to paw your way out.

AU and AW

Dictation 1

Paul hauled the laundry home. There he saw his cat. The cat's paw hit his jaw and cut it because the claws were sharp.

Dictation 2

Kate paused on the way to the barn. The day was raw and the snow was thawing slowly. It did not rain. That might have caused a mess. Then she hauled out the trash can.

AWL and AWN

Dictation 1

At the pass, Sam had a brawl with Tom. He did not let him go on, as it was a dusty trip. He pawned his pin and got cash for lunch. Tom was glad.

Dictation 2

A line of ants was crawling across the lawn. The child was drawn to the sight. She tried to stop them. It did not dawn on her that they might sting. But they did, and she started bawling.

Dictation 3

With daylight saving, the dawn comes later. Dick got up in time, but he yawned and yawned. The birds were on the lawn, hunting for bugs. The dog was bawling at them.

Dictation 4

A stray dog was sprawled on the lawn. "Crawl home, you brat," Dawn drawled. A stranger called, "That is my dog." Dawn pretended to yawn and went into the house. She was not going to be drawn into a brawl.

Dictation 5

Pat was drawn to the window to see Tommy. He was crawling on the lawn after the dog. Then he pushed himself up and started toddling. When it dawned on him what he was doing, he tripped and fell sprawling. He started to bawl and the dog licked him. Then Tommy squared his jaw, took a few steps and bumped into the dog. This time he didn't cry. Pat thought he was finished with crawling.

Dictation 6

Fran sprawled in the shade of a tree, yawning with boredom. A very dull book lay beside her. Suddenly a car came around the corner too fast and shot right up on the lawn. She opened her jaw to bawl out the driver. He was a brawny man, now looking flustered. It dawned on her that she was saved from reading the book. "Have you come to tea?" she said. He grinned.

OU as /ȧu/

Dictation 1

The sound of thunder came loudly. Pat scouted around for shelter.

Dictation 2

Bess found grass sprouting in the ground. Crouching, she counted six, a number to be proud of.

Dictation 3

The cat crouched at the mouse hole, purring loudly. The sound bounded about the house.

Dictation 4

Betty found that each time the man opened his mouth he spouted tripe. So Betty left the house.

Dictation 5

The ground gets soft. The bulbs sprout. The children shout loudly in the yard. The old person stops being grouchy. It is spring.

Dictation 6

A mouse scampered across and crouched under the couch. I shouted in fright. "Count me out," I cried, and bounded onto the bed.

Dictation 7

Jack was proud of the house. He looked around and found it good. Seeds were sprouting in the ground. The only sour note was a mouse in the basement.

Dictation 8

The cat crouched on the ground. In a bound he grabbed the snake and came proudly to Kate with it in his mouth. Kate fished it out carefully, but this did not sour the cat. He liked the game.

Dictation 9

The dog lay on the couch, napping. Joe shouted at him. The dog opened his mouth and yawned. Joe called loudly. The dog turned over and pretended to take a nap. He was too proud to be ordered around.

Dictation 10

I jumped into my car and sped south on the highway. Loud shouts followed me. I was proud of my skill, but this time there was a sour note. I had bungled the job and aroused the man. Well, I must get over the ground fast and get myself hidden before I can count the cash.

Dictation 11

Jim was grouchy. He found that he was bothered by the loud sounds of the boys playing behind the house. He shouted at them and they left on a sour note.

OW as /ȧu/

Dictation 1

How can Val plow now? It is wet.

Dictation 2

How do you plow a driveway without a snowplow? Well, now, by the sweat of your brow, man.

Dictation 3

How did it happen that the cow got stuck? Meg was plowing when she saw the cow crying. Now she stopped and got the cow out.

Dictation 4

The farmer had been plowing all day. As the sun set, he stopped the plow and mopped his brow. Now was the time to quit. How restful was the quiet.

Dictation 5

The cow got into the corn. Now how did it do that? April vowed to find out.

Dictation 6

Don vowed that he was going to plow all day. How foolish. He was not allowed to, for a huge storm came up. How bowed to fate, put the cow in the shed and went inside.

Dictation 7

Sally grabbed the prow of the pram and tried to bring it ashore. The reeds got in the way and didn't allow her to. She plowed along to a sandy strip, got it up and mopped her brow.

Dictation 8

We do not allow the puppy to get into the garden. So when the cow got in and began clumping around, the puppy was mad. He vowed not to let her stay and started to bark. There was quite a row. Now let us all simmer down.

Dictation 9

Fred had a row with Sally. Now how might he cool off? He plowed across the sand, pushed the prow of the boat into the pond, and allowed himself to relax with a fishing rod.

Dictation 10

How the cow got away, no one knew, because it was not endowed with much of a brain. It plodded to the brow of the hill and counted the flies.

Dictation 11

Helen saw the cow in the garden. She lifted her brows and asked, "How in the world did you get there?" The cow looked happily at her and chewed its cud. Helen gave the cow a slight bow and invited it to chew the lilies.

OWL and OWN

Dictation 1

Sam went down the path to town, planning to get a map for his trip. The man was out of maps. Sam frowned.

Dictation 2

Down by the old brown wall the dog growled and the cat howled. Mark scowled and found a rat.

Dictation 3

A loud sound came from the shed. Val ran out of the house and down to the barn and found her horse battering the wall. She was not too proud to howl at a mouse.

Dictation 4

The brown cow tripped down town with a flower in its mouth. It made the dogs growl and the cops howl. The cow did not care.

Dictation 5

The dog was growling at the cat. Pat scowled at him and told him to stop. The cat ran down the street. Pat still frowned at the dog and he pretended to clown around as if he had never seen a cat.

Dictation 6

The town was drenched and almost drowned. Showers fell on the grass and flowers. To crown it all, the wind howled down the streets.

Dictation 7

On the crown of the hill the gray tower stood overlooking the town. When a shower came, it seemed to scowl down at the brown streets and houses.

Dictation 8

Down by the flower beds a snake was coiled to strike. The dog was howling loudly. Mr. Brown frowned grimly and got out a log to strike the snake.

Dictation 9

Tom was clowning around with the dog. His play had too much power. It made the dog howl. The howl soon rose to a growl and the dog crouched, ready to spring. Tom frowned and ran.

Dictation 10

Liz was sprinkling the garden. An oak tree towered over the flower beds. Down by the stone wall the dog was scratching up the new plants. He was howling.

Dictation 11

The child slipped down the street of the little town and stubbed her toe on a rock. She scowled and then started to howl. The dog began to growl. June frowned at the dog. Then, towering over the child, she patted her head and gave her a cone.

Dictation 12

Jack started by clowning in front of the girl, but now he was not joking. He showered her with gifts and crowned it all with a ring. She would not take the ring and they had a whale of a row. He gave up, frowning, and threw in the towel.

Dictation 13

The flower garden was south of the house, down by the barn. The soil was a rich brown and the weeds were a rich green.

Dictation 14

I vowed that I would not allow the puppy to get up on the new couch. How could I prevent it? The puppy made such a row that I bowed to fate and gave up.

OR as /ȯr/

Dictation 1

Tom got his torch and went forth to hunt for frogs. He did not scorn frogs' legs for supper, nor do I.

Dictation 2

The map was torn, but it led Dale on a short path north to the spot. She dug for gold.

Dictation 3

The stork forked a fish in the pond. Sam did not do that well, for he was in bad form. He got a tadpole.

Dictation 4

Ann stuck a fork in the pork. She snorted, for it scorched her mouth. The corn was just as hot and she gave up.

Dictation 5

The storm shook a lot of acorns from the tree. They made a noise as they fell on the porch roof and startled Fred.

Dictation 6

Tom made a fire in order to broil the steak. In a short time he scorched both his hands and the steak and became sort of cross.

Dictation 7

Eve took a short trip north. The sun was scorching hot, the truck was not in good form, and she took the wrong fork in the road. When she got home she was worn out.

Dictation 8

The boy had torn pants and scuffed worn boots. He did not care. He ran around the corner after the stray dog and shortly found himself on a strange porch.

Dictation 9

It was a northeast storm. Fran went out on the porch to see it. Branches were torn from the trees. Acorns pelted the house. Lightning forked across the sky. The storm was short but left enormous disorder.

Dictation 10

Fred was leading his horse when an acorn dropped on him and made him snort. He started jumping about. Fred was worn out keeping him in order, but he shortly rode north and got the horse home.

Dictation 11

Ice formed on a corner of the porch and made a worn spot. When it began to thaw, Peg had a grand time standing under the drip. Jen had to break it off in order to keep it from dropping and hitting her.

Dictation 12

The spy knew he was being followed and might be stopped at the border. The train was speeding north. At a patch of deep woods he pulled the cord and jumped off as it slowed down.

Dictation 13

I went into the bathroom in order to brush my teeth and saw a stork in the tub. I snorted in astonishment. The stork gave me a scornful look, got up in a portly way and stormed forth from the house. It vanished to the north.

Dictation 14

Jim was riding his horse when a thunderstorm overtook him. He formed the intention of getting in out of the wet. He saw an old shack and hitched his horse to the porch. Inside he found a torn rug and some worn-out chairs. He made a fire and scorched his fingers.

Dictation 15

Kim drove north around a corner and found a horse in her way. She honked her horn. The horse did not budge. In order to pass it, Kim had to go a short way over the curb. A worn spot in a tire gave way and she had a flat.

An Idea Used Four Times

CHAPTER 6

You may want to postpone **ge** and **dge**.

Withstand and **notwithstanding** may be omitted if they are not in the student's vocabulary. On the other hand, they offer the opportunity to increase vocabulary, which all of these students need.

Exercise 1 — page 45

speck	stock	flock	stake
stroke	blink	beak	mark
black	like	brisk	tack
mink	dark	buck	
luck	duck	tank	

Exercise 4 — page 46

cracker	chicken	bracket	tackle
market	ticklish	locket	stinker
ticket	darken	packet	
pickle	slicker	cockpit	
sparkle	tanker	banker	

Exercise 5 — page 47

pink	blank	tickle	mask
tack	speck	brisk	reckless
bake	cricket	park	speak
truck	beak	silk	
chicken	spank	hockey	

Exercise 6 — page 47

suck	sulk	bunk	leak
spoke	plank	pork	struck
link	racket	stack	
lick	flock	blank	
bracket	strike	lock	

Exercise 7 — page 48

hatch	clutch	latch	etch
trench	pitch	stretch	patch
ditch	bench	munch	drench
ranch			

Exercise 8 — page 48

march	scratch	itch	slouch
pitch	lunch	stench	hitchhike
scorch	poach	preach	satchel
crouch	catch	matchless	winch

Exercise 9 — page 49

speech	rich	sandwich	snatch
hunch	coach	pitcher	pitchfork
notch	kitchen	porch	

Exercise 10 — page 49

lunch	stitch	much	punch
which	teach	latch	torch
ouch	cockroach	Dutch	Scotch
scorch	ratchet	such	

Exercise 11 — page 50

dodge	bridge	gouge	forge
binge	badge	ridge	large
range	fringe	rage	drudge

Exercise 12 — page 50

edge	dredge	plunge	wedge
charge	barge	budge	bulge
stooge	binge	twinge	
trudge	ledge	change	

Exercise 13 — page 50

gorge	widget	budget	indulge
cage	lodger	ridge	strange
badger	cringe	cartridge	tinge
fudge			

Exercise 14 — page 51

partridge	ledge	porridge
change	fidget	cringe
fledgeling	bilge	smudge
singe		

K and CK

Dictation 1

The child picked up the rock and dropped it on her foot. She got mad and kicked it.

Dictation 2

Ted tucked his lunch in a basket and stuck it in the truck. He took his fishing tackle and drove briskly to the sand for a day in the sun.

Dictation 3

Jake picked up his change and dropped it into his pocket. Then he took the ticket and tucked it into his billfold.

Dictation 4

Miko put on a pink silk dress, stuck her ticket in her pocketbook and went to town.

Dictation 5

Beth took a bucket of swill to the pig. The porker was sulking in the muck, but it got up briskly and began eating at a shocking rate.

Dictation 6

Jill lay on her back on a blanket by the lake. She saw a flock of ducks. She picked up a rock and tossed it, but had no luck. She lacked the skill to wake a duck.

Dictation 7

The puppy hopped onto the blanket and started getting muddy spots on it. Beth asked the puppy to get off. The next moment it got back on. Beth gave up and put the puppy in the kitchen.

Dictation 8

The lock on my truck's door was jammed. I tried to pick it, but no luck. I was in a pickle, for my delivery was going to be late.

Dictation 9

Jack lost his ticket. It slipped down a hole in his jacket pocket. He ran around quacking like a duck. What a racket! Then he became sulky. Joe told him to look in the lining of his jacket and he found it.

Dictation 10

Jack took a pork sandwich and some milk and pickles and went to the pond. He ate his lunch and then lay down on a blanket in a patch of sun to get tanned.

Dictation 11

In the bushes by the bank I found some cash. I yelled for help and people flocked out of the bank. A person with a badge grabbed me. I was in a pickle.

Dictation 12

It was dusk. Mark sat in an old rocker on the porch. The crickets were making a great racket. The sunset was pink in the west. As it grew dark, the fireflies began to sparkle.

Dictation 13

After the plane took off, the hijacker went into the cockpit and made the pilot fly to Cuba. There was a shortage of gas, so the pilot had to land in Florida. Planes were stacked up over the airport because it was fogged in. They finally landed and the man was stuck in jail.

Dictation 14

It was so cold that the gas pumps froze. The wind was brisk and biting. My breath looked like smoke. The truck did not start. The burner picked that time to go out.

Dictation 15

I got a pink ticket for the hockey game and stuck it in my pocket. Then I went briskly to the parking lot and slipped out to the highway. The trees sparkled in the setting sun. I slowed down, for it was reckless to go fast in the dusk. The crickets sounded loud in the blanket of darkness.

Dictation 16

Sparked by all the lights and decorations, Janet tackled the problem of Christmas gifts. Putting on a thick jacket, she went briskly into a store. The prices were shockingly high. She wasn't that reckless, so she dickered and got them down. She came home with a mound of bulky packages.

CH and TCH

Dictation 1

Pat struck a match and lit the fire. Then she stretched out on the couch and munched on a sandwich.

Dictation 2

Dale scorched the toast. She drenched it in butter, poached the eggs and had her lunch.

Dictation 3

Jim was hiking up the hill to the notch and skidded on a slippery patch of ground. To keep from falling he snatched at a branch.

Dictation 4

Mark hitched a ride home. He was cold. Crouching by the fire, he scorched his jacket. Then he stretched out on the couch.

Dictation 5

June saw a cockroach in the kitchen. She snatched it up in a paper and drenched it in the sink. Tossing it out onto a patch of muddy grass, she began to get lunch.

Dictation 6

There was a bang in the night. Kate snatched her torch and went to look. She had a hunch it was a witch.

Dictation 7

Mark felt grouchy and sleepy. He snatched a cup of coffee and hurried home in the rain. He got drenched and was crosser than ever. He stretched out on the couch to catch a nap.

Dictation 8

Jack felt grouchy. His wool sweater was scratchy. His coat had a patch on one sleeve. His boots pinched his toes. At lunch time he went home and changed everything.

Dictation 9

Tom chuckled when he saw the chicken stretching its neck to catch the corn. It had a scrawny neck and thin cheeks. It was a charming sight.

Dictation 10

Martha slipped into the kitchen to snatch a cup of coffee. The cat was scratching to get out. She let it out into the muddy March day.

Dictation 11

The batter marched to the bag. He clutched the bat. When the ball came over the plate he stretched and gave it a sharp rap, right past the pitcher into left. A man snatched at it, but did not catch it. He made a home run.

Dictation 12

Mary had poached eggs for lunch. She drenched them in butter. Munching toast, she slouched over to the window to see the March sun on a patch of March mud. She slouched back and stretched out to catch a nap.

Dictation 13

Helen was lying in bed when she heard a noise. She stretched out to get her torch, trying to catch sight of something. It was nothing but the cat, crouching in a corner sniffing at a cockroach.

Dictation 14

Crouched in the bushes, Jane looked for a buck. With a torch in her hand, she was a skillful poacher. She knew that jacking a deer is unlawful, but she was bound she was going to catch one. She ought to be arrested.

Dictation 15

The storm was bad. Jake had a hunch it might get better. A patch of blue showed. He snatched that time to go out to lunch. But he was mistaken and got drenched. It made him grouchy.

Dictation 16

Sam, crouching behind the handlebars of the bike and clutching them tightly, pretended he was winning a great event. The crowd was shouting and clapping and calling his name. It was a fine moment. Then he struck a patch of oil, skidded and fell. All was quiet. There was nobody there but an old cockroach. The dream was ended.

Dictation 17

Sally looked out of the kitchen window to see what the day was like. The snow, which the wind was blowing, had banked up high. It was much colder. Sally munched on a sandwich and then stretched out on the couch to catch a nap.

Dictation 18

The cowboy was looking for the poacher. He found him crouching in a ditch with the stolen sheep. He marched him to the clink. Then he hitched up his belt, carved a notch on his gun, and rode out to catch more poachers.

GE and DGE

Dictation 1

The fire was so large that Tom singed his finger. He staged a big fuss and trudged inside to get a plaster.

Dictation 2

Val was in a rage. She had a fight and bore a grudge. She swore she was right and did not budge.

Dictation 3

Hope slipped on the edge of the bridge and fell. It left a large smudge on her pants.

Dictation 4

Mark plunged into the apple grove. He gorged himself on the apples until he had a twinge of pain. He had a large binge.

Dictation 5

Roy did not like the job. It was drudgery and the wages were low. Planning to change it, he became so happy that he went on a large binge.

Dictation 6

Marge barged into the store and got a paper. She stuck the change in her bulging pocket. When she plunged her hand into the pocket, all the coins fell out. She felt like a fool.

Dictation 7

Nan had a lodger. He forged a check. He tried to dodge the cops by plunging into the crowd, but they got him.

Dictation 8

Marge was driving her truck too fast and barged into the bridge. She plunged over the side into the drink. She was able to back out, but it made her raging made.

Dictation 9

Paul had a grudge. He felt his wages were not as large as they might be. He plunged into a rage and charged the boss with being nasty. The boss did not budge.

Dictation 10

The boy on the bike skidded to the edge of the pond by the bridge. His mouth bulged with gum. The pond was tinged with red from the setting sun. He saw a large fish and barged in to catch it.

Dictation 11

The day was damp and the man had twinges in his bones. He trudged over the bridge to town, limping a little. His dog dodged in and out of the shrubbery, ranging about in the woods and plunging into the pond after a tadpole.

Dictation 12

Dan and Fred had a grudge fight. Dan called Fred a stooge and Fred called Dan a badger. Then they plunged in. Dan dodged Fred, and Fred dodged Dan. What a silly sight.

Dictation 13

April charged up the hill in her truck, dodging the rocks at the edge of the street. She plunged over the bridge and got stalled. This put her in a rage and she indulged in strong words.

Dictation 14

Madge was mad at the world. She felt like indulging herself, so she forged a large check and gorged herself on food and drink. When the police got her, she did not grudge the binge. It was money well spent.

Dictation 15

Indulging her sweet tooth, Pat went on a binge and gorged herself on ice cream. Then she got into her car, dodged traffic, drove across the bridge and went over a large bump with a twinge of fear. The fear was justified. She found herself using a widget to change a flat tire.

K and CK, CH and TCH

Martha made a pork sandwich, snatched a jar of pickles and slipped off to the beach. She picked a patch of shade and sat munching her lunch while she watched the gulls basking in the sun. A cat watched her, lurking in the tall grass and crouching alertly. Suddenly it sprang at a bird and the flock wheeled into the air with matchless grace, making a racket with their cries.

K and CK, CH and TCH, GE and DGE

Fred took the boys to the bridge. They skidded down a notch, clutching at branches and getting scratched. He found three men hunched over fishing rods, trying to catch fish and munching blades of grass. He told them that there were other fishing holes, but that this was the best swimming hole in the river. They were grouchy, but they snatched up the rods and slouched away. Then he tied a rope to a plank in the bridge. The boys stood on the rock, latched onto the rope, swung out over the river, and dropped in.

Words ending in BLE, DLE, etc.

Dictation 1

The boy slipped on a pebble and stumbled into a puddle. He hit his ankle and dropped his bundle. He had to hobble home.

Dictation 2

Jim took his rifle. He juggled a pebble and shot at it. But he bungled the job and hit a tree.

Dictation 3

Betty stumbled down the marble hall in the dark and banged into the wall. Her elbow started to tingle and her ankle throbbed. She was worn to a frazzle.

Dictation 4

Barb paddled the pram to the sand. She got her bundle of sandwiches and settled in a shady spot with a bottle of milk.

Dictation 5

Jack was needling Marge and chuckling at her and getting her muddled. Marge got mad and tackled him. Jack got rattled and buckled under the blows. Then they had a bottle of coke.

Dictation 6

Thunder rumbled in the sky and made me tremble. Mark was a trifle frightened also, but he had to set an example. He chuckled and cried, "This is fun."

Dictation 7

Ben hobbled over to get his coffee kettle, and put it on the fire. He grumbled a bit at the cold, but soon cuddled in his blanket and watched the fire.

Dictation 8

The broken bottle sparkled in the sun. I started to handle it, made a muddle of it and cut my finger.

Dictation 9

A drizzle quietly ruffled the leaves in the woods. A single turtle made ripples in the water as it settled to the pond's bottom. This is simple beauty.

Dictation 10

Jack struggled to get beyond the tangle of underbrush. His fishing rod got stuck and made him stumble. At last he was able to get to the pond. He was feeling a trifle tired.

Dictation 11

Ann was carrying a glass of milk. She stumbled on the rug, bobbled it, and almost dropped it. While she juggled it, she started to giggle. She set the glass on the table and huddled on the couch, struggling to stifle her giggles.

Dictation 12

Frank ladled out the soup and gave his little poodle a bone. He settled down to his simple supper. Then he ambled outside, nibbling a cracker, and the dog paddled after him. It was not so stifling hot in the garden.

Endings

CHAPTER 7

Exercises 5 and 6 — pages 60 and 61

boastfully	wastefully	sorrowfully
spitefully	lawfully	fretfully
joyfully	masterfully	hopefully

Exercise 7 — pages 61 and 62

delightfully	usefully	tactfully	pitifully
respectfully	painfully	tunefully	fancifully
shamefully	carefully	dreadfully	mercifully

Exercise 8 — page 63

lightly	widely	gravely	steadily
totally	completely	luckily	crazily
extremely	safely	heavily	healthily
lately			

gently	ably	sensibly	cuddly
singly	drizzly	humbly	doubly

NG

Dictation 1

We are longing to ring the bell that hangs in the tower. We will have to bring a ladder and go up rung by rung.

Dictation 2

She was hungry and ate some food to bring up her strength. She ate with a fork, not with her fingers.

Dictation 3

I was shingling the house. I bungled it and hammered my finger with all my strength. It gave me a pang.

Dictation 4

There was a noise the length of the street. A thrush was singing in a tangle of bushes. A hungry dog was barking for a bone. Fran felt the spring also. She broke into song and began beating time with her foot.

Dictation 5

Bob strung a length of rope from the porch to a tree. It slipped across his fingers and burned them. He hung his pants on it and the strong wind dried them.

Dictation 6

Beth went up the rungs of the ladder and started to hang up a string of lights. A bee stung her, bringing a loud cry and making her angry. She got all tangled up.

Dictation 7

Fred was stringing up a length of yellow lights. His fingers got tangled in it. He became very angry and almost strangled.

Dictation 8

The hungry rat ran the length of the dump, but the package of bread got tangled in the underbrush. The angry rat flung himself out of there with all his strength.

Dictation 9

Mark went up the ladder, bringing a bucket of paint with him. He filled in the chinks in the wall with the brush but he was strung out so far that the paint can overturned. It was a king-sized mess.

Dictation 10

Ted and Fran planned a picnic. Fran had a strong hunch that it might be bungled. The string on the package of food broke. They were so hungry, that they ate it anyway, dirt and all. Then a bee stung Ted's finger. The air rang with his yells.

NK

Dictation 1

Rose sank down on a blanket on the sand. She started to drink some cold coke. Thanks to her brother, she had a good lunch.

Dictation 2

I think I have twisted my ankle. I will sit on a blanket in the sun and rest it. When the pink sun sinks in the west, the ankle will be better, thank you.

Dictation 3

Frank took some junk to the dump. It was a stinky place. Old cans and bottles winked in the sunlight and twinkled when stuff was tossed on top of them. Frank blinked at the sight.

Dictation 4

Thanks to a sunken rock, Fred twisted his ankle. Looking blankly at it, he sank quickly onto a grassy bank and started rubbing it. He had to hobble home and it made him cranky.

Dictation 5

The girl had neat ankles. She seemed to twinkle as she went down the street. Sam blinked at the sight and gave her a wink. She gave him a wink back.

Dictation 6

A car honked right behind Paul. He flung himself onto the bank to get out of the way. His foot sank into a hole and he twisted his ankle.

Dictation 7

Ann put a length of string around the newspapers and took them to the junk yard. The sun was sinking and she blinked in the strong light. Then she drank some coke and ate a hunk of cheese.

Dictation 8

I spilled my drink on the blanket. I crinkled it and put it in the washer. I cranked the washer on and hoped that the pink soda would not leave a stain.

LESS and NESS

Dictation 1

It was a thankless job to clean out the barn. It seemed endless. It was very hot under the pitiless sun.

Dictation 2

The sky seemed to stretch endlessly over the sea. The sunset's brightness was blindingly beautiful. This priceless sight brought us such happiness.

Dictation 3

His endless kindness during my illness was striking. It was hopeless to try to thank him.

Dictation 4

The cow stood in the grass, tirelessly flicking off flies. Now and then she chewed her cud.

Dictation 5

It was hopeless to try to have a garden. The puppy dug holes in it endlessly. But there was no meanness in him. He ran up breathlessly to lick Jane's hand.

Dictation 6

Dan's illness lasted a long time but he was not hopeless. It was pointless to worry. Instead he happily watched the tree outside his window turn from buds to countless leaves.

Dictation 7

Meg worked tirelessly for the candidate. It was a thankless job. She didn't get the votes.

Dictation 8

The homeless dog was not used to kindness. It had known only meanness all its life. Ted tried endlessly to tame it, but it was pointless to go on.

Dictation 9

The cat picked up the lifeless body of the bird and in all kindness brought it to Jim. It was pointless to tell her he did not want this mindless gift. She knew he did.

Dictation 10

Happiness is little things: the smokeless air, the countless kindnesses you meet, the thickness of a steak, the breathless asking of a child, the readiness to help in illness, the thankful loneliness of a tramp in the woods.

Dictation 11

The barn was so cluttered that it was hopeless to find the Ping-Pong set and even pointless to try. As Tom came to this conclusion, he saw the old basketball hoop and the bow and arrows. His time was well spent, after all.

Dictation 12

The day was hopelessly bad. The fog was endless. The wind was pitiless. It was a good thing Helen was not homeless. She made a fire and forgot the day.

Dictation 13

Dale got hopelessly lost in the endless snow. It was pointless to try to make a fire. The thickness of her jacket kept out the cold and saved her from illness.

Dictation 14

To Martha the road seemed endless. In her kindness and readiness to help she had taken on a thankless task. She was hopelessly depressed. Suddenly a partridge darted out of the woods and ran into her car. She stopped and picked up the lifeless body and began to look more depressed. There was no happiness for Martha this day.

FUL and LY

Dictation 1

The puppy playfully ran after the ball. Swiftly he dropped it at Tom's feet. He was really being helpful.

Dictation 2

The drawing was freely and boldly drawn. The playful puppy helpfully snatched it and ripped it. It was totally ruined.

Dictation 3

The boys had a fight. They traded blows freely and swiftly. Tom boldly hit Mark very hard and really got the upper hand.

Dictation 4

Dawn was blissfully happy. Her pants were ripped and her hands and feet were totally muddy. She ran swiftly across the yard, boldly running after a large but playful dog.

Dictation 5

It was delightfully cool and crisp. Fred stepped out boldly and ran swiftly down the hill. The wind helpfully pushed him along. It really might be harder running home into the wind.

Dictation 6

Linda was totally right in thinking that New York City was too big. Planes flew boldly and swiftly above. It was really delightful to visit.

Dictation 7

I closely followed the weather forecast. They boldly said the weather was going to be fine. They were largely mistaken. It really snowed.

Dictation 8

Joe rode the playful horse carefully down the highway. He came to the top of the hill and had a really fine look at the sight. It was simply a sunny day in spring.

Dictation 9

Pam was trying to clean up the large old barn. It was a thankless job. Rusty tools lay in a pile. The leftovers of a lifetime were scattered about. In fact, it was simply hopeless.

Dictation 10

Jack drove swiftly down the street, playfully waving to all the girls and boldly honking his horn. We say freely that this is not really helpful. Yes, he crashed into a tree.

Dictation 11

The child was quietly playing on the grass when a powerful car splashed wet mud on him. It was totally disgraceful. The child was fearful and finally started to cry.

LE and LY

Dictation 1

Jake simply dropped his cake, so he sensibly let the dog eat it.

Dictation 2

There was simply no time to spare. Meg gently spurred her horse and got to the train on time. It was probably the wildest ride she ever had.

The Y Rule

CHAPTER 8

Exercise 1 — page 66

happiness	trying
spied	fried
tinier	drying

Exercise 2 — page 67

prayer	spying	carried	payably
easily	heaviness	crazily	glorious
readiness	buyer	craziest	hurrying
healthiest			

Exercise 3 — page 68

noisiest	player	joyful	tried
noisily	steadiness	carrying	sleepiness
worrying	lazily	supplied	enjoyable
daily	destroyed	payment	copying

Exercise 4 — pages 68 and 69

dismayed	employment	merriest	furious
drying	envious	funniest	hurrying
shied	supplying	injurious	dutiful
melodious	brayed	multiplying	annoyed
appliance	smokiness	craftiness	

The Y Rule

Dictation 1

Tim hurried to the store, praying not to be late. Happily it was still open and he got some food.

Dictation 2

Now came the joyful spring. The sun was higher and hotter and bills were payable.

Dictation 3

The child was carrying a cone. It was melting fast in the sun and dripping all over. She tried to lick it before it spilled. Then it dropped to the ground and she cried furiously.

Dictation 4

Dan made a payment on the car. He hurried to get gas and tried out the speed.

Dictation 5

Marge was spying out the land. The pitiless sun shone on her. Happily she saw a pond and got a drink.

Dictation 6

The child strayed into the ditch. It cried. The dog's bark carried far. Jim hurried over and got the child out.

Dictation 7

Jane got a bill. She was dismayed to find that it was payable on the tenth. Happily she had cash in the bank.

Dictation 8

Sam copied the list. He tried to do it well and enjoyed the job.

Dictation 9

Jane hurried out of the shop. It was an enjoyable fall day. Luckily, it was not cold.

Dictation 10

Pat was carrying milk to the playful puppy. Luckily, it did not spill. She patted the puppy happily.

Dictation 11

Jane got the bill, but she delayed payment until her next check came. She tried to be careful about charging.

Dictation 12

It was a hot day. We were playing in the sprinkler and shouting joyfully. The puppy tried to play also, but the kitty stayed out.

Dictation 13

Jane was humming happily as she whipped the batter. She carried the cake to the stove and slipped it in to bake, saying merrily that it had better be good. It was a most enjoyable supper.

Dictation 14

Dan was going skin-diving, but he stopped to fish. He tried to get a playful fish. It carried on a glorious fight. Dan muttered a prayer and luckily got the fish.

Dictation 15

It was getting dark and the fogginess was thick. Tom was worried about his dog. Carrying his flashlight, he tried to find him. Luckily the dog barked.

Dictation 16

Jones carried his letters inside. He was dismayed to find a big bill from the drugstore. He stopped worrying about it and made a payment by check.

Dictation 17

Peg tried to study, but her brother was frying eggs and the baby was crying. Luckily the baby went to sleep and her brother sat down to eat. Studying was now enjoyable.

Dictation 18

Fred was wakeful. The moonlight shone dimly in the window. The cat was whining. Fred was nervous and got up noiselessly, stepping softly. There was no robber.

Dictation 19

Bugs were destroying the plants, so Mark started spraying the garden. His dog hurried to see what was going on and got a dose of spray. Luckily, it did no harm.

Dictation 20

Dale made a payment on the hi-fi and carried it home. She got a lot of enjoyment out of it. It had a glorious sound.

Dictation 21

It was a glorious fall day. Dawn was hiking up the hill, carrying a lunch. She hurried to make a fire and cook the hot dogs. When it began to rain, she was not worried. She stayed under a tree until it stopped.

Dictation 22

Liz hurried out from work. It was a most enjoyable fall day. There was a smokiness in the sky. The trees were glorious.

Dictation 23

They were playing the hose steadily on the burning house, spraying the roof. They tried to put the fire out, but the smokiness make the job hard.

Dictation 24

The fire caused smokiness in the air. Mark was dismayed and delayed going to work. Luckily the fire did not come his way.

Dictation 25

Frank saw the boy playing in the grass. He started running and tripped and fell. He cried and cried. Frank carried him into the house and gave him candy. It was the easiest thing to do.

Dictation 26

Clam chowder is better if it rests a while. Tom carried the great pot out to the table in the shade. Everybody happily crowded around and ate with enjoyment. Everyone passing by sniffed the smell enviously.

Dictation 27

The easiest way to stop worrying is to think furiously of something else. Frank turned his mind to the enjoyment of nature, picturing the glorious morning, with the birds singing happily.

Dictation 28

It was a glorious afternoon so Robin went out. The sun was shining, a puppy was barking furiously, the cars were honking joyously, the children were playing noisily and the ducks were quacking industriously. It was the easiest thing in the world to stop hurrying and worrying.

Dictation 29

The child was playing happily with the hose, enjoying herself. Hope got sprayed but she was not dismayed. Luckily she had on an old shirt. When the child turned the hose steadily on her car, that was carrying things too far. Hope hurried over and easily stopped her.

Dictation 30

Spying on the boy, Ann saw jam on his pants and on the table. He was smiling happily. It was an enjoyable sight.

Dictation 31

The child was playing noisily in the next room. Then all was mysteriously quiet. Dan was dismayed and spied on her. The girl was happily making cakes with crackers and jam. What a mess!

Dictation 32

Sam delayed getting his supplies. He did not want to start laying brick until the weather was better. On a glorious day he hurried to begin.

Dictation 33

One of Pam's hobbies was her grass. She worried about it because it was getting yellow. While she prayed for rain, she sprayed it, hoping to make it healthier. When the rain came, it was a joyful day. She hurried home to enjoy it.

Dictation 34

Sam was drying the glasses the easiest way he knew how. He was trying to go fast. A glass slipped and broke noisily. He was the sorriest when he saw that it was his best wine glass.

Dictation 35

One of Rose's hobbies was collecting stamps. Everybody supplied her with them. She had an enormous amount but luckily she was not dismayed. She worked happily away and steadily added to her collection.

All Three Rules

Dictation 1

Don slipped happily away from work and trotted smilingly down to the beach. The lazy sea gulls were noisy. The sand was getting hot. He found a shady spot and shamelessly relaxed with a little nap.

Dictation 2

The heavy snow blotted out the sky. The trains were late. The wind slugged the waiting people and ripped at the shutters. Mopping-up operations were disgracefully slow. It was worrying to think how damaging the melting snow would be.

Dictation 3

The storm was the worst in New England's history. No one was equipped to tackle it. Trains were derailed, upsetting thousands. Roofs fell in with the weight of the snow. Road equipment received a lot of damage. Cars skidded and stalled. A bridge caved in crazily. Businesses sent their employees home. Stores ran out of supplies. Luckily, it stayed fairly warm.

Vowel Digraphs

CHAPTER 9

OW as /ō/

Dictation 1

The sparrow sat in the window, showing off. Then it hopped to a little hollow in the shadow of the tree and got a bug.

Dictation 2

The fire showed a glow. Yellow light flowed into the room.

Dictation 3

The yellow flowers made shadows on the wall. The wind was blowing the branches beside the narrow path. As it began to grow dark, the light flowed from the windows.

Dictation 4

The fellow drifted down the narrow lane like a shadow and slipped into the house by way of the window. The cop saw the glow of his flashlight and stopped him.

Dictation 5

The cat came slowly down the lane, following the bird. It went like a shadow. The bird sat on a windowsill. The cat jumped up but the bird was quick. It flew to a hollow tree.

Dictation 6

The fellow was shadowing us. He followed us around all day. We did not know how to shake him off.

Dictation 7

The moon shone yellow in the narrow street. Rose was frightened by the shadows and followed the glowing light thrown from the windows.

Dictation 8

The fire glowed with a soft yellow light, making flickering shadows in the trees. It was growing dark. A light wind was blowing and ashes drifted like snow. It was time to broil the steak.

Dictation 9

The snow showed the tracks of the sparrows on the narrow path. Now and then they skidded. I followed them before the wind could blow them away.

Dictation 10

I peeped in the window. The room was in shadow, but the glow of the yellow street light showed that no one was inside. I started to go in, but a slow footstep sounded in the narrow road and I had to hide.

Dictation 11

Tomorrow the president will throw out the first ball and baseball will begin in a happy glow. As the shadows grow, the advantage will be with the pitchers. A pitcher's duel will likely follow.

Dictation 12

The child was playing with her bow and arrow. She tried to hit a tree and narrowly missed a sparrow. But she did not miss the window. It was quite a blow. It followed that her father was angry.

Dictation 13

I went out of the window and something followed me. I ran fast. The yellow light cast my shadow on the wall. I darted like an arrow, but I was too slow. The dog nabbed me.

Dictation 14

Beth looked out of the window. The grass was dry and yellow. Snow still lay in hollows on the north side of the house. But the buds were slowly growing fat. The glowing sky showed that it was spring.

EA as /ē/

Dictation 1

The diner was clean and the meal was cheap and good. Jean had a cup of steaming tea.

Dictation 2

I have been reading about, and speaking with people who make tea, from tea leaves. It isn't easy research, but I enjoy it.

Dictation 3

The sky was clear. Down by the beach the air was clean. Sneaking away from class, Bob retreated to the shore. He took a bag of peanuts and lounged at his ease on the sand.

Dictation 4

If Pam cheats on her income tax she will be teased by bad dreams. She will be cheap and sneaky. There will be a leak. It is easier to lead a clean life.

Dictation 5

Please do not tease the beasts. Clean the cages. Make the place neat. Put the trash in a heap in the rear. Let the animals squeak and squeal. Treat them well. You will reach your dream of a nice clean zoo that will appeal to everybody.

Dictation 6

Tom had an ear for sound. He liked what he called the cheap stuff but he enjoyed hearing other kinds also. He taped records. This was not cheating. He always got consent.

Dictation 7

Linda sneaked away and went to the stream to fish. She dreamed of quiet but the woods were noisy. A bird got a worm in its beak and had a feast. Linda finally got a fish and landed it neatly.

Dictation 8

The man sneaked a cheap TV set out of the department. It was a neat job and he might have got clear away. A cop saw him. In fear he leaped out of the window and ripped the seat of his pants. That will teach him!

Dictation 9

Lead me to the hill country. It is easy to reach and the leaves are stunning in the fall. The car is a cheap little heap, but it will get us there. Do not bring the dog. It has fleas. I repeat, it has fleas and fleas like me better each year.

Dictation 10

The meat was cheap but the man cheated on the weight by sneaking in some extra fat. Mary was far from pleased. That is the reason that leads her to go to another market.

EA as /ĕ/

Dictation 1

Rose was ready to go ahead with the trip. The weather was good. She left right after breakfast.

Dictation 2

In summer we have pleasant weather. Sometimes the air gets heavy and damp and we have to put on a sweater.

Dictation 3

Jack had no weapon to protect himself from the attacking snake. He grabbed a log and dealt it a heavy blow. Death came quickly, but it was a dreadful sight.

Dictation 4

The hills were dead ahead. Jean threaded her way south. Meadows spread around her. She took a healthy hike and got home hungry.

Dictation 5

I was fishing in my pram. Suddenly dead ahead of me was a large ship. Sweat started on my brow. It was a dreadful moment. I threaded my way around it.

Dictation 6

The ship had all sails spread, but it looked like heavy weather ahead. We were in a sweat to get them down. Then the heavens split and the storm came.

Dictation 7

The weather was heavy with rain. It spread over the town. After breakfast Sally put on a sweater and went out. Dan wanted her to stay inside instead, but she went ahead anyway.

Dictation 8

Heavy clouds spread across the sky. The weather was threatening and the air was like lead. Frank was deaf to all this. He put on a sweat shirt and went out for a healthy jog.

Dictation 9

Frank took pleasure in the fine fall weather. He dragged on a sweater and was ready for a hike. A thread from his sweater stuck on a thorn and it ripped. That is when it began to rain.

Dictation 10

After breakfast Pat went out to spread lime on the lawn. The weather was heavenly. It was a pleasure to handle the soil. She worked up a healthy sweat and was ready for a shower.

Dictation 11

Because it was good weather, Mary dragged on her heavy sweater and took a tramp over the meadow. She had a sandwich of bread and meat. It was a heavenly day and she took long breaths of the delightful air.

Dictation 12

The weather was way below freezing. An arctic air mass had spread over New England. Tom wore an extra heavy sweater under his leather coat and a cap with ear flaps on his head. He was ready for the cold. He meant to go ahead and hike across the meadow. He was a nut about his health.

EA as /ā/

Dictation 1

It is a great day to break away for a drive. Do not tear down the road too fast. Better wear a jacket.

Dictation 2

Dale started to wear her oilskins, but they were hot. She went outside. After the storm, it was a great day to look at the wild breakers.

Dictation 3

The breakers flowed up the beach, tearing up the sand to the cliff. Frank carried the steaks. Val was breaking sticks to make a fire.

Dictation 4

The steaks looked great, but Ted found that it was not tender. He had to tear at it with his teeth. He was afraid he might break one.

Dictation 5

The bear bothered the beehive and got stung. It made a break into the woods at great speed, tearing at the sting with its paw.

Dictation 6

That is a great shirt. Do not wear it while you change your winter tires. I swear you will tear it.

Dictation 7

It is a great day for a cook-out. The breakers pound the beach and sooner or later will wear down the bluff. Let's tear up this dead branch, make a fire, and broil the steaks.

EA as /ē/, /ĕ/, and /ā/

The dog tried to scratch a flea and hit a great heap of dishes. They started to break and made a dreadful noise. He had no mean streak and was frightened. Jane was not angry. Instead, she cleaned up the mess.

OO as /ü/

Dictation 1

The room was cool and pale in the moonlight. The little girl stooped and looked in. It was spooky. She was no fool and did not choose to enter.

Dictation 2

The schoolboy fell off his bike and into the swimming pool. He felt very foolish.

Dictation 3

After school Jill stepped up to the lunch booth and got a hot dog and some root beer. Then she went swimming in the pool. It was too soon after eating and she got cramps. She was foolish.

Dictation 4

Dave dropped his tools gloomily on the porch and sat down on a stool. Three days after Easter and it was snowing! Well, he might as well get some food. He went back into the room to heat the coffee.

Dictation 5

Putting a useful stool at the window, Roy looked outside. At noon the day was tiresomely cool and gloomy. Roy felt hopelessly cooped up.

Dictation 6

At noon when the children got out of school, they all trooped up to the booth to get the football tickets. It was quite a crush. A boy booted Sal. She fell down and broke a tooth. It was a foolish thing to do.

Dictation 7

The flowers are blooming and soon the radishes will be ripe. Jake likes to grow some of his food and still has room in his garden for bulbs. He roots out the weeds and the shoots of crabgrass and smooths the soil between the rows.

Dictation 8

The poor girl was running so fast that she tripped and fell into the pool. Her boots filled with water and pulled her down. Foolishly, she struggled. Finally, she pushed up from the bottom and grabbed the rail.

OO as /ů/

Dictation 1

Jack saw the crook hide behind the woodpile. He looked shook up. Jack saw what was cooking and looked for the police.

Dictation 2

April hooked a fish, got a lot of wood, made a fire and cooked it.

Dictation 3

Jan understood that the fish were biting in the brook. She took her rod and went to see for herself. She came back later with three trout that she cooked for dinner.

Dictation 4

I took a good look at the fresh spring day. The brook was chattering its way noisily through the woods. A small child was playing in it and getting drenched. I understood the temptation and almost went wading myself.

Dictation 5

Dan was going to see his girl and tried to put his best foot forward. He put on his good jacket. His tie was a trifle crooked. He shook his head to lay it flat. He was ready.

AI as /ā/

Dictation 1

Faith was running to catch the train. She failed to see a large nail and tripped on it, spraining her ankle. She almost fainted with pain. Yes, she missed the train.

Dictation 2

A man has broken out of jail and the trail comes this way. Remain quiet and do not faint. We hope to restrain him. The main thing is not to raise a rumpus.

Dictation 3

The rain plunged down the drainpipe and rushed across the lawn, making a faint trail in the snow and raising the point that it might freeze on the road.

Dictation 4

Ted tried to steal a car. He failed and was stopped by the police. He was taken to jail and was denied bail.

Dictation 5

The rain was coming in beside the drain and staining Edith's bedroom ceiling. She tried to catch it in a pail, but that failed. Using her brains, she nailed the bucket outside, and that worked.

Dictation 6

Jake was detained at the train waiting for his mail. He finally claimed his mail, and went to the main lumber store in town, to get a pail of paint. He failed at raising any help. What a wait!

Dictation 7

Where the train crossed the plain there were rocks. Dick failed to be careful and stumbled over one. He felt a sharp pain in his ankle and thought it was sprained. It was silly to remain there, waiting for help. He started back at a snail's pace, telling his brain not to faint on the way.

AY as /ā/

Dictation 1

Down by the bay Faith went swimming with the boys. The waves sprayed the rocks and a stray dog barked.

Dictation 2

The dog was out playing and strayed away, for she was a very gay dog. Dan heard her braying near the dump and prayed she would not be harmed.

Dictation 3

It was May and the display of spring flowers was very gay. Frank sprayed them carefully. His dog played around for a time and then strayed off.

Dictation 4

The day was bright. The rays of the sun were hot. The roses were gay. Pat stayed away from work and strayed out to the lake.

Dictation 5

The cat stayed out all night. I suppose she was hungry. I relayed the message to the kitchen. She got a great plateful of food. Then she began frisking playfully.

Dictation 6

There has been a delay. The speaker will be late. Pray do not display your anger. I may say it makes me mad. If she cannot stay and make up the time, we will not pay her.

Dictation 7

I will stay in bed today. My cold is bad. You may say that I am a slippery faker, but that will not slay me. Bring me a tray of food, and do not delay. I am hungry.

Dictation 8

It was the day the big football game was to be played. There was a delay when a dog strayed out and began barking. A message was relayed to the timekeeper while the players rounded up the dog. It was a better show than the game.

EE as /ē/

Dictation 1

Cheer up, you creep, and lift your feet. We will sweep down the street at full speed. Just remember to steer!

Dictation 2

Meet me on Main Street and we will get seeds to make the garden green. We had better get stuff to feed it, too.

Dictation 3

A sweet spring breeze was blowing down the street. Jim felt it sweep across his cheek. It made him sleepy.

Dictation 4

Last week it seemed like fall. Now it feels like winter. The trees are bare. The wind speeds the clouds across the sky. It is freezing cold.

Dictation 5

Sam peeped at the beehive. A bee started to follow him. He ran fleetly down the street, screeching. What he needed was a screen.

Dictation 6

The week seemed to go with the speed of light. It was a degree below freezing. Everyone agreed that the weather was strange.

Dictation 7

Pete and Bee took the boat from the creek. They planned to seek a spot to go skin diving. They rowed over the green waves and were greeted by a keen wind. It seemed freezing and they went home.

Dictation 8

Lee started to sweep the kitchen with good cheer. A light breeze was creeping through the screen. The air was sweet, his cheeks were pink and his feet were jigging. Indeed, it made him feel grand.

Dictation 9

I need to feed the cat. She greets me with a cry. After she eats, she speeds down the street, full of pep, with heels flying. She creeps after birds, but they will not stay to be snatched. They flee from her.

Dictation 10

It was ninety degrees and very muggy. The air smelled sweet but felt sticky. Ants were creeping along a steep bank. Bees were buzzing and birds were cheeping in the trees.

Dictation 11

The street has a steep downgrade. The wind sweeping along the trees at a speed of twenty-five miles has a queer moaning sound. The seeds are up. Let us hope it does not freeze.

Dictation 12

Fred was a greedy boy. Between lunch and dinner he went to the canteen and speedily stuffed himself. He ate a cheese sandwich and had a sweet drink. His cheeks were bulging.

Dictation 13

Dee was speeding down the hill when she almost hit the sheep. She felt a degree of astonishment. What indeed was it doing on the main street? It got up and breezed off.

Dictation 14

The sleepy little village looked cheerful in the summer breeze. Sheep were grazing in the green meadows. The sweet smell of clover hung in the air. Indeed, the village seemed as if it had escaped the human greed.

OA as /ō/

Dictation 1

Don had a load of coal for the winter. On the road home the truck stopped. He let out a groan.

Dictation 2

A toad croaked beside the road, boasting loudly. Joan saw her new boat floating at the dock and gloated over it. She was as bad as the toad.

Dictation 3

Jack went fishing on the coast. He got soaked in the rain but he did not mind. He had a load of fish and left the frogs croaking on the foaming shore.

Dictation 4

The storm roared out of the northeast, making the waves foam and the trees groan. The wind moaned along the coast. Bits of wood and even boats were torn away and floated on the sea.

Dictation 5

The boat floated on the lake. The goat stepped off the sand and tried to get in. The load was too much and the pram tipped over. Ted let out an oath.

Dictation 6

Pat heard moaning and groaning floating in the air. She found a goat huddled in the bushes. She shouted hoarsely for help.

Dictation 7

My farm chore was to take a load of oats to the barn, for the foal. When I got to the barn, there was no foal. The foal had roamed off to her favorite oak tree.

Dictation 8

Sam was floating happily along the coast in the pram. The boat sprang a leak and he got soaked. As the water began to foam around him, he groaned. He stopped loafing and started rowing. His goal was to land before he sank.

Dictation 9

May woke up with a hoarse groan in her ears. She got up and roamed about the house. Her goal was to find what was moaning and groaning. It was no witch, just Billy snoring.

Homonyms

CHAPTER 10

Nothing is needed in the Teacher's Manual to accompany **Chapter 10.**

More Word Patterns

CHAPTER 11

When you teach the silent letters **(kn, wr)**, go over the list in the dictionary, so the student will know that they are strong patterns.

Words like PUT /u̇/

Dictation 1

Hide behind the bushes and pull the trigger. Do not put a bullet in the bull. That can hardly be helpful.

Dictation 2

Mark pulled up the weeds and put them with the trash in the bushel basket. It was soon full. Then he clipped the bushes, but he butchered them.

Dictation 3

The baby pulled the pudding off the table. What a mess. After her father put a clean blouse on her, she did it again.

Dictation 4

Pam was a bully. She pulled a fast one by putting a spoonful of salt in Jean's coffee. Pam would have yelled at her, so she ran out and hid in the bushes.

Dictation 5

The butcher cheerfully pulled out his best meat for Jim. It cost a bushel of money, but Jim gratefully paid.

Dictation 6

Marge had a bushel basket full of trash. She pulled up at the dump and started throwing the trash over the edge. I stood there with a gun, waiting to put a bullet into any rat that showed up.

Dictation 7

Sally stole some apples from the trees and put them in a bushel basket. She pulled the trunk of the car open and pushed them inside. She felt that the farmer might be hiding in the bushes, and he was. She was caught.

Dictation 8

I pulled the trigger and tried to shoot the tin can. The bullet went wild and hit the bull hidden in the bushes. I felt like a butcher. The bull came charging out and luckily pushed past me. I got out of there fast.

Dictation 9

Jane pushed the window up. She saw that the bull was cheerfully grazing. She leaned out the window and over the bushes to pat the bull. The bull ignored her and trotted away.

Dictation 10

I put a cheerful yellow ribbon on my white pussy cat and pushed it out of the house. It wove in and out of the bushes. When it returned, its coat was full of little twigs and the ribbon was filthy.

Words like MOTHER /ŭ/

Dictation 1

January was a very cold month. It was wonderful to cover up and stay inside. There was not much snow to shovel.

Dictation 2

Pay day had finally come. Among other things, Joan wondered what she would spend her money on. She had a dozen different ideas. Joan loved to spend money.

Dictation 3

Ray sailed to the fort. They shoved off at seven. In front of them were docks to tie up the boat. Above was the fort, a wonderful thing.

Dictation 4

On Monday a storm covered the ground with snow. It looked lovely but was somewhat hard to shovel. The comfort is than in another month it will be March.

Dictation 5

It was a fine day in the month of May. Val got her glove and a dozen balls and started playing catch with her brother. Nobody won, but they had a good time.

Dictation 6

It was wonderful what someone had done with the old car. It took a lot of cash and much loving care. The seat was covered with the right color and the front was polished. Brother, what a job!

Dictation 7

On Monday the snow cover was melting fast. On Friday came the big storm. Dick looked above at the dark clouds. Oh, well, it was only ten inches. He smothered his feelings and began to shovel.

Dictation 8

After Mom shoveled out the barn, she took a sponge and mopped the windows. For a while, there was nothing more to do. Trying to smother a yawn, she settled down in a shady spot to catch a nap.

Dictation 9

The lights went out. James wondered what to do. It was some comfort that the phone still worked. This governed his actions. He called the company and lit some candles. They said somebody would come right away.

Dictation 10

Monday was a bad day. Nothing was done right. Somebody shoved Monday's newspaper into the trash. The milk was covered with ants. The heat was above ninety. It is a wonder the dog did not bite the postman.

Dictation 11

It was stormy, but Paul liked that. He put on one comfortable jacket, for he never smothered himself in a dozen layers. He pulled on some gloves, covered his head with a cap and shoved off. Everything was a gray color. Fog rose among the trees. He had a grand time. When he got home, he put his boots in the oven to dry.

Dictation 12

Sometimes Jack was lucky. On Monday he got a call from his son Mark. The car had skidded on an oil slick, but everybody was all right. Jack wondered about that and went to see for himself. All they had were a dozen bumps.

Dictation 13

On Monday I covered myself with glory. I stood up in front of the class and gave a wonderful report. I shone above many others. Nothing could equal me. There was agreement among all that I had won the prize.

Dictation 14

Nan shoved an apple into her pocket and went out of the house, wondering what to do. Nothing seemed like fun. Suddenly a monster with two heads and a long tail slipped up and grabbed her apple. She ran after it with a shovel and struck her lovely red apple out of its paw. It ran away and she ate the apple.

Dictation 15

It was the muddy month of March. Puddles covered the grass. Melting snow dripped from the roof above. Nothing could be gloomier, but somebody shoved a bright yellow plastic rose into the mud. There is hope.

Dictation 16

One Monday morning in the month of May Jack found himself with nothing to do. The sky was a lovely blue. The shrubs were covered with flowers. Wonderful smells came from somebody's garden. Just like that, he took off for New Hampshire.

Hard and Soft C

Dictation 1

The city may be the center of life, but not when you are broke. Bob did not have a cent left. He took a pencil and wrote home for cash.

Dictation 2

Mr. Jones decided to go into the club to smoke a cigar and drink a glass of cider. He had to ring the bell twice.

Dictation 3

Dee had a choice of space and decided to settle near the center of the big window. There was a cold draft and she took a cup of coffee rather than a glass of cider.

Dictation 4

Alice had a glass of cider. She liked it better than a citrus drink. Looking out of the window at the falling snow, she decided to stay home. She put a log on the cinders and settled down.

Dictation 5

Beth was trying to write a letter. The pencil broke twice. The coffee got cold. Books were taking up a lot of space. The room was so tiny it was like a cell. Well, that is the way the cookie crumbles.

Dictation 6

It was cold and damp in the old camp. Jack lit a candle and made a fire. In the center of the decaying junk he found a bottle of cider. He sat on a bench by the fire, clasping the cider. The old bench crashed and so did the bottle.

Hard and Soft G

Dictation 1

The dog was a giant, but she was very gentle. She was a gem of a hunter. It seemed like magic.

Dictation 2

It was a giant bug and it waged a gem of a battle with an ant in the grass. I was glad when the gentle bug escaped.

Dictation 3

June was engaged in sweeping the trash out of the gutter. She plunged into the job when she got good and ready. There was no magic about it, just hard work. She got very grimy and had to change her clothes.

Dictation 4

The gypsy lounged on the fringe of the crowd, planning to pick pockets. George saw his game. The gypsy gently snatched a gem from a man and slipped along the gutter. George gritted his teeth and followed him grimly.

Dictation 5

May found the Model A motor in the junk yard. She wiped the cinders gently from the grimy thing. It was a gem. She decided to clean it up and use it to pump water from the lake to the kitchen.

Words like YOUNG /ŭ/

Dictation 1

Roy took the trouble to bring his young dog into the country. He slipped on the wet grass and fell down. The dog touched him with his nose.

Dictation 2

Mr. and Mrs. Young went into the country to see the spring. It was a touching sight. The couple had trouble with their car and got home late.

Dictation 3

The morning was young and in the country the fall was glorious. The sunlight touched the trees to flaming reds and yellows. The wind made it doubly bright by rippling the shining river. It was a valley of light.

Dictation 4

"Can you lend me a couple of bucks? I do not like having to ask, but I have to go into the country."

"Yes, if you can wait a bit."

"All right. The day is still young."

Dictation 5

The raging storm got the young trees on the southern side of the street. They were bent double by the snow. A couple had been broken. The snow was dry and light and fell at a touch. It was not much trouble to free the trees.

Dictation 6

I went to visit my cousin in the southern part of the state. She lives in the country and has a couple of horses. We went riding. Once we got into trouble because we rode too far and it started raining.

Dictation 7

The morning was young and the air was fresh. A light breeze made it doubly invigorating. Spring was coming to the country. I played a couple of rounds of golf before going to work.

Silent K (KN)

Dictation 1

Mark was playing with a knife. It slipped and cut his knee. He knew he had been foolish.

Dictation 2

I knocked. The house was silent. I fiddled with the knob, but it was locked. I knew no one was home.

Dictation 3

The puppy jumped on the little boy and knocked him down. He fell and skinned his knee. He did not know the puppy was playing and started to cry.

Dictation 4

Barb knocked but felt that there was no one home. She fumbled with the knob and knelt down to look in the crack, but could see nothing. She tied a knot in the string and hung a note there.

Dictation 5

Jill took her knife and carved her name into the wood. She knew she had to be careful, but she got the knack of it quickly.

Dictation 6

Frank got a knot in the string and did not know how to untie it. Then he took a knife and cut it.

Dictation 7

I saw the child with the knife. I knew he might cut himself and he did. He was knotted up with pain. I knocked it out of his hand and picked him up.

Dictation 8

Every boy knows how to play mumblety-peg. Do not let the knife slip. It might hit your knee, not the ground. Before you start, knock on wood.

Dictation 9

Ben saw the boy playing with a knife. He knew it might slip. A puppy jumped up and knocked it out of his hand. It cut his knee.

Dictation 10

The knob did not turn, so Pam got down on her knees to look through the keyhold. There was no light, so she knew no one was home. She would have to go through a window.

52

Dictation 11

Jack had a knack for sailing. He knew how to tie knots and never had to cut them with a knife. Knock on wood. He might, the next time.

Dictation 12

Frank was carving with his knife. He accidently dropped it, and the knife hit his knee. He knotted his tie around his leg to stop the bleeding. It is lucky he knew what to do.

Dictation 13

I knocked off work because it was a bright day in spring. I put on my knapsack and went for a hike. I had a knack for spotting odd things. I thought I saw a fossil in a rock. How to get it out was a knotty problem. I pried it out with my knife and came home with a rather knobby knapsack.

Silent W (WR)

Dictation 1

Jack got a gift from his girl. He wrapped up the package and wrote a letter to go with it. By that time he was a wreck.

Dictation 2

Pat took a wrong turn, skidded and wrecked the car. She wrapped a bandage around her wrist and wrote a report.

Dictation 3

Jack wrapped the package, but he wrote the wrong street number on it. It was sent back to him to write the right one.

Dictation 4

Nan was a bad driver. She did everything wrong. She wrapped her car around a pole and wrecked it. She broke her wrist and had to stop writing.

Dictation 5

The boy bothered Paul when he was writing. He was taking things and hiding them. He wrecked the desk. Paul felt like wringing his neck.

Dictation 6

Jack wrapped the package and wrote the name and street on it. Then he got into his wreck of a car and drove to the mailbox. He took the wrong road and got lost.

Dictation 7

Taking a wrong turn on his bike, Frank rammed into a tree. He broke his wrist. He was not able to write, even when he wrapped it tight.

Dictation 8

The child wrapped the package and made a wreck of it. She wrote the name, but it was the wrong one. Then she dropped it and started to cry. Fran helped her with it, tied on a big bow, and sent her cheerfully on her way.

Dictation 9

Jan was riding in the car with Beth. Beth hit a tree and wrecked the car. Beth wrenched her back. She wrote it off to carelessness.

Dictation 10

With a flick of my wrist, I threw my knife into the tree trunk. Then I wrote my name on it. You wretch! It was the wrong thing to do. That can wreck a tree.

Dictation 11

Mark slipped on a curve and crashed into a tree. The car was a wreck. He wrenched his back and sprained his wrist. It was a wretched way to end the day. He wrote a report for the Registry.

More Endings

CHAPTER 12

AGE

Dictation 1

The little girl managed to drop her toast. Pat put it in the garbage. A savage dog came along and tipped over the garbage can to get the toast.

Dictation 2

Bill stuck the rest of his old lunch in the garbage. A savage dog got it.

Dictation 3

The sea gull made a voyage around the dump, looking for garbage. It found a package of old bread. Before the bird could salvage the bread, a savage rat managed to grab it.

Dictation 4

Carl had cabbage for lunch and then left the summer cottage to take a message for his mother down to the village. As there was a shortage of fresh bread, his mother wanted the man to save a loaf for him. He picked up a package of crackers to take its place.

Dictation 5

Jane made a passage by boat to the cape. The voyage was long and there was a shortage of water. What did she do?

Dictation 6

Snow fell on the cottage until it was snowbound. The wind whiped savagely around it. No one got out. Tom phoned a message to the village store that he had a shortage of bread and milk.

Dictation 7

The average person likes corned beef and cabbage and maybe a glass of beer for supper. Janet left a message asking her husband to cook some on Friday.

Dictation 8

Tom managed to burn the toast and Jane tossed it into the garbage. He got the message and was more careful.

Dictation 9

The savage storm damaged many cottages in the village. The river overflowed its banks and ravaged the farms. There were shortages in everything. Everybody managed by helping each other.

Dictation 10

Beth was staying for the summer in a cottage outside a little village, when a savage storm blew in. It caused a lot of damage. After the passage of the storm she sent a message home that she was all right.

Dictation 11

Dead and stinking cabbage leaves littered the ground of the cottage. Jake left a message for Grant that if he did not put his garbage in the can he would call city hall. Grant spoke savagely. "That is compost."

Dictation 12

The violent storm ravaged the city. After its passage Ann went out to see the damage. The cottage had lost part of the roof. Almost everything was broken. She rummaged around in the mess, using some very strong language.

Dictation 13

Fred was in a savage mood. He hated the smell of cabbage cooking in the kitchen. He stumbled and hit the pot and damaged his arm. He did not need a bandage, but he did need an outlet for his temper. He slipped the cabbage into the garbage can and felt better.

WARD

Dictation 1

"Onward and upward toward the top," shouted someone.

Dictation 2

As Dave went southward, he hunted for a diner. He did not find a spot to eat and turned homeward for food.

Dictation 3

On the seaward side of the house there was a grand sight of sky, waves and clouds. Northward, toward the road, was a grove of trees.

Dictation 4

Nan stumbled and slid downward toward a black hole. Inwardly she was frightened. Outwardly she stayed cool and grabbed a shrub. That stopped her. She went homeward thankfully.

Dictation 5

Beth looked northward toward the hills and started hiking. Soon she found herself on a cliff that stretched sharply downward. She would have to go around it on her way homeward.

Dictation 6

As Liz went slowly homeward by the woods, she looked downward at the path. A snake slithered toward her. It was a harmless garter snake. She picked it up and went onward.

Dictation 7

The gull went upward on a homeward flight. Mark leaned forward to see it. He felt an inward kinship toward the bird, as if he could glide and fly also.

Dictation 8

Bee was going homeward in the snow. Looking downward, she saw a striking gold pin. She picked it up and went back toward the school and into the office. They said she could have it if no one claimed it.

Dictation 9

I was looking forward to getting a great haul from the bank. The coins made an awkward clanking sound. I looked backward, saw the police and was sunk. I wound up in the clink.

TION /shŭn/

Dictation 1

Kate was bored. Then she got a notion and went into action. She went to the station to see the train go by.

Dictation 2

The police officer motioned to the drivers to slow down. They payed attention and showed caution, for there was not much traction in the snow.

Dictation 3

Do not mention snow to me. It is piled so high at the edge of the road that you can not see the cars. At the station the trains are mobbed.

Dictation 4

The motion of Jim's car was too fast and it hit the car ahead of him. Jim had no notion how it happened. The police took the men to the station.

Dictation 5

Mary went to South Station to catch the train. She had a notion to go to New York. That is where the action is.

Dictation 6

Tom went to the station to meet Fred. He drove with caution, for the road was slippery and the tires had very little traction.

Dictation 7

Pam had a notion that there was a bad fire. Sirens screamed. In addition, she saw a lot of smoke. Fire fighters came and went into action.

Dictation 8

Ben made a motion to show that he was in a rush. The action got the attention of the girl. She mentioned that she had a car. Ben liked the notion and soon they were driving to the station.

Dictation 9

Paul was late at the station, for he could not get traction on the hill in the snow. The rubber tires did not function well. It caused a lot of emotion. Yes, he missed the train.

Dictation 10

There was friction between Ann and Mary over a dress. Ann had a notion that if she paid no attention to Mary's emotional outbreak and did not mention the dress, the commotion would quiet down.

Dictation 11

Betty had a notion that the station was southwest. Her action in going left took her in another direction. In addition, her car stalled. Did I mention that she was angry?

Dictation 12

The fire truck left the station in a hurry. It got a lot of attention. It could not get any traction on the slick street and skidded into a store, causing quite a commotion. The driver should have used more caution.

Dictation 13

People were gathered at the station. A car came along. A child stepped onto the tracks. Dale grabbed him and saved his life. Her action got the attention of everyone. That night it got the attention of the nation on TV.

Dictation 14

There was friction in the shop, reflecting a lot of emotion. Pam turned her back on the commotion and gave her attention to her work. Someone had to function as usual.

SION /zhŭn/

Dictation 1

There was an explosion in the barn. In the confusion Dan got hit. He was not badly harmed.

Dictation 2

If a blackout happened, there was little provision for extra power. Tom had a vision of the confusion that would result.

Dictation 3

Marge went to the station. She came to the conclusion that the train was late. It led to much confusion. Marge had a vision of missing her dinner.

Dictation 4

There was an explosion at the school. Windows were shattered. In the confusion some children were cut. The teachers came to the conclusion that everybody must go home.

Dictation 5

The fire truck was in collision with a window. There was an explosion and a lot of confusion. There was an invasion of sightseers. Everybody had a different version of the occasion.

Dictation 6

We were having a fight when an invasion of biting fleas caused a diversion. In the confusion we stopped fighting and came to the conclusion that we should get a coke.

Dictation 7

As Joan rode her bike down the hill, she had a vision of delight. She dreamed of Thanksgiving dinner. Then she had a collision with a tree and an invasion of reality. I mean she banged her head.

Dictation 8

Fran made an excursion into the woods, but it was not much fun. An invasion of ants got into the provisions. In the confusion they bit her and caused an explosion of temper. She came to the conclusion that she did not care for picnics.

TION and SION

Dictation 1

The explosion was very loud. It shook the ground. In addition, it caused confusion. The people at the fire station went into action.

Dictation 2

Mark had a notion to make an excursion to the ball park. He stationed himself where the vision was good and gave his attention to the game. When the catcher hit a home run there was great emotion and an explosion of noise.

TURE

Dictation 1

The cows were in the pasture, eating a mixture of clover and grass. They made a fine picture. Tom's interest was captured and he started to sketch them.

Dictation 2

The structure was a mixture of old and new. Moisture had damaged the walls. The light fixtures were hanging crazily. The windows were punctured by rocks. It was a sad picture.

Dictation 3

The mixture of heat and moisture in the air was torture. Linda tried to capture the fleeting breeze. She decided that in the future the only solution to this high temperature would be departure.

Dictation 4

The structure was shaky. The fixtures were old and grimy. The furniture was shabby. The departure of the children left it lonely.

Dictation 5

Jake did not think of the future. It was not in his nature to picture bad luck. He simply went from one adventure to the next. For most of us life is a mixture of good and bad.

Dictation 6

The town was a mixture of cultures. It had houses with thick walls that are found in Mexico. These structures were cool in the summer when the temperature went up high. People need to think of nature in the way they live.

Dictation 7

There was moisture in the pasture. Liz slipped and fell and thought she had fractured her ankle. She was the picture of dismay. There was no one around. How could she make her departure without help? She tried to get up and had no trouble. The structure of the ankle was perfect. So she picked some wild flowers and went home.

Dictation 8

Bob was asked to lecture to the men. His nature was not bold, and he felt a mixture of pride and fright. He wished he might fracture a leg and get out of it. Time passed quickly and he was tortured. Moisture gathered on his brow. He made himself do it and captured the crowd. It was quite an adventure.

Word Building

CHAPTER 13

When you come to Latin roots in the reading, use them for word building.

It is surprising how many of these words are in the students' vocabulary. Most older students are familiar with such things as a protractor, a transistor radio, and a trajectory.

The students may know all of the words listed on pages 103-105 or below. Tailor the lesson to their vocabulary. Endings can be varied: **ing, tion, ance, ed,** etc.

Port

comport	opportunity
deport	report
disport	support
export	transport
import	

Mit and **mis**

admit	admission	
commit	commission	committee
	dismiss	
emit	emission	
intermittent	intermission	
omit	omission	
permit	permission	
remit	remiss	remission
submit	submission	
transmit	transmission	

Pose

compose
depose
dispose
expose
impose
interpose

oppose
propose
repose
suppose
transpose

Script and **scrib**

ascribe
conscript
describe
inscribe
prescribe
proscribe
subscribe
transcribe
script
scribble

description
inscription
prescription

Fect

affect
confection
defect

effect
infect
perfect

Tract

attract
contract
detract
distract
extract

protractor
retract
subtract
tractor

Spect

aspect
disrespect
expect
inspect

prospect
respect
suspect

Ways to Spell ər

CHAPTER 14

WOR

Dictation 1

What in the world are you working on? I am working on a crossword puzzle. Is it worth doing? Don't worry, it is fun.

Dictation 2

Sam's boss had some harsh words to say about his work. The worm turned, and Sam swore at him. He lost his job, but it was worth it.

Dictation 3

Dawn was worried about the house. It was run-down and getting worse. If she fixed it up, it might be worth quite a lot.

Dictation 4

For what it is worth, here is an old saying: the early bird catches the worm. It is not a very worldly idea.

Dictation 5

What in the world was that? Dick saw something glittering. He worked it free and picked it up. It was a ring. Was it worth anything? That didn't worry him. He polished it and put it on.

Dictation 6

Her work took her all over the world. It was hardly worth it to have a house. But she was not a worrying person and just forgot it.

Dictation 7

Ann was worried about working in the heat. As the day went on it got worse and worse. She decided to quit. She felt like a worm, but it wasn't worth it to go on.

Dictation 8

A penny is not worth much today. What in the world can you do with it? It gets worse and worse. You work, but what do you get?

Dictation 9

Don got the word that the world was coming to an end. He was not worried because he did not think it very likely. Just in case it did, he quit work and managed to have some fun.

Dictation 10

I liked the pin, but it worried me because it was worth a lot. If it worked free and dropped off, I would feel it in the worst way. The word was to be careful.

Dictation 11

Working in the morning, Danny had the worst fright. He was driving the jeep in and Jack almost slammed into him. What in the world got into him? The jeep was worth a lot.

Dictation 12

The members were worried about the house of worship. Worms were making holes in the woodwork. They did not know what in the world to do. Ms. Smith said, "Do nothing. The worm holes make it worth more, for they show how old it is."

Dictation 13

Pam knew that one good spot for fishing is Cape Cod. It was the worst kind of weather, but that did not worry her. Pam got some worms, worked her way across the sand to the shore, and began casting for all she was worth.

EAR

Dictation 1

Mary heard the dog barking and learned that there had been a robbery. The cops searched high and low, but they did not find the string of pearls.

Dictation 2

Early in the morning Dave heard the foghorn. The earth was folded in pearly-gray mist. He had to drive in it to his job or else he would not earn his living.

Dictation 3

The early bird gets the worm. He searches until he finds it. He earns it the hard way, by tugging and pulling.

Dictation 4

Fred earned his living by getting up early and searching in the sand for coins dropped by swimmers. He had learned long ago that the beach has riches.

Dictation 5

Jan heard the cries and earnestly searched in the bushes until she found the monster. She put a bandage on his cut and earned his gratitude. Early the next morning he gave her a pearl.

Dictation 6

Early in her life Sally learned that she liked to do research. She earned her living at it in many spots on this earth.

Dictation 7

Pat was in earnest about learning the code. She worked at it early and late. When the teacher heard her, the teacher said that Pat had earned a good mark.

Dictation 8

Dick planned to take his pal on a trip. He got up early, when the earth was fresh and bright, and picked his pal up. She dropped her pearl ring in the car. They heard it land, but they searched all over and did not find it.

Dictation 9

Have you heard the latest? A little boy is lost. They are searching all over for him. They learned about it early in the morning and started as soon as it was light.

You haven't heard the rest. Where on earth have you been? He was found in his own bathroom.

Dictation 10

Jack heard the storm in the night. He got up early, thinking that the waves might have left interesting things on the sand. He went out to search for shells and pebbles.

Dictation 11

Barb went to work early, in search of a good parking spot. She had learned not to park in an unlawful spot because she got tickets. But where on earth was room to be found?

Dictation 12

In the early morning the black hearse went quietly down the street. It stopped on the turnpike. A man hopped out and lifted the hood. When he heard the armored car come charging down the pike, he got out a gun and stopped in earnest. Three other men left the hearse with guns and the resulting hold-up showed plenty of rehearsal. Police searched the earth for the loot but learned nothing.

ER

Dictation 1

The herd of cows got nervous and trampled the grass. The farmers shouted at them in strong terms.

Dictation 2

It made Fred nervous to see his little sister perched that high in the tree. There was a very strong wind. It might jerk her off the branch. He got her to come down.

Dictation 3

Jane's brother made her lunch. She thanked him and took it to work. She drove in because she did not like to be herded on the subway.

Dictation 4

The child was perched on the porch rail. The barking dog served to make her nervous and she started to fall. Tom jerked her back safely.

Dictation 5

A termite is bigger than a germ, but a germ makes Dale more nervous. It works internally. That is worse.

Dictation 6

Kate started to serve coffee but she hit the fern with her elbow. It fell and broke the pot. She felt like a jerk.

Dictation 7

There was a herd of cattle in the meadow. A bird perched on one of the cows and made it nervous. It jerked its ears, but did not get rid of it. Then the bird saw a worm and left the cow alone.

Dictation 8

Termites are quiet, but they must make you nervous. They can do more internal damage than a herd of thundering bulls.

Dictation 9

Wade perched himself on a hill under some tall timber. Far off the hills merged into a green backdrop. He saw a herd of cows to his left. Down below his family was in the yard, picking flowers and ferns for the house.

Dictation 10

Jane went across the fertile meadow, where a herd of cattle was chewing the ferns. As she passed one of the cows jerked its head up. Jane got nervous. She charged along quickly to the verge of the grass and straddled the fence. The cow didn't care.

Dictation 11

Bill's dad served lunch in the garden. Birds perched in the trees. Bees buzzed about the cake. Ants gathered around the cold chicken. The ice cream melted in the hot sun. It was a perfect day. Everyone went home early.

IR

Dictation 1

The girl was thirsty. She got a drink of coke and dripped it on her shirt. A bird was chirping at her from a tree. She said, "Bird, don't scold me."

Dictation 2

When you are thirsty, the first thing to do is to find a drink. Jake asked a girl and she told him how to get it himself.

Dictation 3

The girl sat on a bench in a green skirt. The wind stirred her long hair. She saw Ben and said firmly, "I am thirsty." It was a neat way to start flirting.

Dictation 4

The girl had been hiking. Her shirt and skirt were dirty, but she did not care. She saw a man hosing his grass. "Sir, I am thirsty. May I have a drink?" she asked. He smiled and fetched a glass.

Dictation 5

Mark had been camping. The first day he hiked thirty miles. On the third day his shirt was so dirty that he went home to get clean and eat a sirloin steak.

Dictation 6

Nan saw the bird lying on the path. At first she began to think it was dead, but it stirred and fluttered its wings. The girl picked it up, thinking it might be thirsty, and took it to a puddle. The bird started chirping and hopped away. Nan shook the dirt out of her skirt and hopped away too.

Dictation 7

When Ted found the third shirt he picked up to be dirty, he was stirred to anger. The firm that did the shirts was thirty years old, but its work was getting careless.

Dictation 8

After work Tom put on a clean shirt and went to his pal's house. It was her twenty-first birthday. He gave her a pin. It wasn't worth a great deal, but she liked it.

UR

Dictation 1

On Thursday there was a purple smog. On Friday you burned with the heat. On Saturday the rain curled your hair.

Dictation 2

The church burned down. Purple smoke and red flames rose from it. Nobody was hurt. By Saturday they had a purse pledged to do it over.

Dictation 3

On Thursday a turtle was cast up on the sand by the strong surf. He landed with a gurgle and turned to go back in. A sea gull saw him and hurled at him.

Dictation 4

On Saturday Bill took a boat ride. The sky was purple with clouds. The wind burned his ears. The surf was wild. It was murder. He quickly went ashore.

Dictation 5

On Thursday Beth burned her hand. By Saturday it had turned purple and hurt very much. She had to quit work and get it treated.

Dictation 6

Marge was nursing a cold. On Thursday she went to town. Turning right at the red brick church. she parked the car and went to the drug store. She got some pills to help her fever.

Dictation 7

What a nice surprise it was when the nurse said I could go home on Saturday. All of a sudden, my leg didn't hurt anymore.

Dictation 8

There was a purple turtle with a curly tail. It took him from Thursday to Saturday to go from the barn to the pond, ambling along at his own speed. He was spurred by a need for water.

Dictation 9

The nurse lived in the suburbs. On Saturday a man was murdered and his purse was stolen. The police were spurred to action. So was the nurse. She turned purple with fright.

Dictation 10

The murder took place on Thursday in the suburb of Charlestown. The snowstorm furnished a clue, as there were tracks in the snow. The newspapers urged a quick solution. Surprisingly, by Saturday the cops had got their man.

Plurals, Possessives, Contractions

CHAPTER 15

Exercise 1 — pages 111 and 112

is	am	not	would
is	will	are	not
would	not	have	
had	not	not	

Exercise 2 — page 112

not	has	not	will
will	not	not	has
not	have	is	will
have	will	is	have

The Open Syllable

$$\bar{A}$$

Dictation 1

The man was a faker. He tricked the old lady into taking her savings out of the bank. She was crazy to do it. Fred saw it happen and stopped the man.

Dictation 2

Dale was raving mad. She had put her savings on the table while she ladled out some soup. When she looked, some shady faker had taken them. Dale was crazy to do that.

Dictation 3

The baker stuck a table and some stools on the paving by his shop. He sold buns and coffee and little cakes and added to his savings.

Dictation 4

I spaded the garden and started raking up the trimmings. Then I got lazy. Finding a vacant spot under a shady tree, I began reading the paper.

Dictation 5

May was a lazy lady. She did not like baking nor scrubbing the basin, nor setting the table. She did not mind ladling out the soup. She would rather find a shady spot and read the paper.

Dictation 6

David was lazy. He kept raving about how he was saving to get a skin-diving outfit, but he didn't even have a job. He was a crazy faker.

Dictation 7

In a shady spot under a tree I was making ice cream. The children helped to turn the handle. When it was ready, daylight was fading. I put the bucket on the table and ladled out the ice cream. At last it was quiet while they ate.

Ē

Dictation 1

Jim had a dark secret. He was scared of females. What an idea!

Dictation 2

In the garden of Eden there was no evil.

Dictation 3

Fran liked to be with fun people. This boy looked like fun. She relayed her message with a wink. He relayed it right back.

Dictation 4

The girl was a charming female. Mark was no hero, but he felt equal to anything. He made no secret of his delight. He asked her to have a coke with him.

Dictation 5

Linda had a secret plan to blow up the bank. She was in a fever to get started. The defect was that she could not hide her gadget. The bank teller stopped her and became a hero.

Dictation 6

Jan had an idea that something had happened at home. She was in a fever to get there. The demon of worry was pushing her needlessly. When she got home, all was quiet.

Dictation 7

Jill thought she had a fever. The red line went up to 103 degrees. She felt awful. Her mother smiled and told her the secret. There was a defect in it. Jill got well quite quickly.

Dictation 8

June liked the idea of having secrets and relaying them to her friends, but even she could not find very much to say until she saw the hero of the recent football game at the corner store sale. Nothing could equal her excitement. She was in a fever to tell someone all about it.

Dictation 9

The boat was sinking. Paul feverishly relayed the message in secret code and a destroyer came. Paul did not feel like a hero, but the females had the idea that he was equal to anything.

Dictation 10

Billy saw the kitten floundering around in the waves, clinging to some driftwood. He rowed out in the storm in a feverish hurry to get it. The sequel to this heroic little exploit was that he got his name in the paper. After all that, no one wanted the kitten.

Dictation 11

Dave had a secret idea that all females were demons. Then he skidded on a curve and sent his car crashing down a bank beside the road. A girl stopped her car and helped him out of the wreck. She took him to a doctor and even relayed a message to a gas station to get a tow truck. Really, this female seemed to be a decent sort.

Dictation 12

A large group intended to go to the top of the hill. Secretly Tom considered that the defect in this plan was that some of the people may not all be equal for the task. It would be an evil thing if they were left behind. His idea was to pick a smaller hill. Everyone would have called him a demon.

Ī

Dictation 1
Petunia was driving to a diner to have a quiet supper. She found a spider in the soup. Luckily, she was not on a meatless diet.

Dictation 2
The sniper took a trial shot at the plane with his rifle. The flier made a spiral dive and got out of the way. It was a trifle risky.

Dictation 3
Dan was driving along the highway, looking for a diner. When he saw one he stopped, but he was going fast and skidded into a tree. After that he was minus a car.

Dictation 4
The tiger stepped into the diner. Everyone was startled. She looked over the items of food, sniffed, and went out. There was no crisis.

Dictation 5
The storm went from Idaho over Iowa and into Ohio. It was a tiger of a storm, causing great damage and a crisis in every town.

Dictation 6
Meg went into the diner to get some dinner. She found a spider in her soup. After that she could not digest her food. She left minus her dinner, but she wasn't hungry any more.

Dictation 7
Jack was an expert driver. He drove skillfully over the road clogged with snow. He took his rifle along and tried to shoot some game. Unhappily, there were no tigers.

Dictation 8
Jane went to tidy the kitchen and found some spiders. There was no crisis. She picked them up in a paper towel and put them down the drain. The climax came when she found another in the hall. What a riot!

Dictation 9
Driving in a snow squall, Frank skidded on a curve. The car went flying and he went diving into a snow bank. When he picked himself up he found the car toppled against a roadside diner. He was all right but he was minus transportation.

Dictation 10
The item in the paper said, "Triumph to the Miners." I wondered who their rivals had been.

Ō

Dictation 1
Jay donated his time to the program, for he was interested in teaching boys how to swim.

Dictation 2
Fran dropped the glass and it crashed. She went poking about to locate all of the broken bits. She was not going to let the boys be harmed. It is no joking matter to step on glass with bare feet.

Dictation 3
Clem looked for Roy and located him in the park, riding a pony. Before he had spoken, the boy fell onto the stony ground. Clem ran to him, but nothing was broken.

Dictation 4

Marge fixed her attention on the boy. He had a perfect profile. As a bonus, he had red hair. She openly admired him.

Dictation 5

When we were going down the hill, we smelled something smoking. We went poking around until we found it. We splashed the fire, saving the day. Later, we got a bonus.

Dictation 6

The boy was the focus of all. The girls were buzzing around him like locusts. It took Fran a moment to locate him. He was openly giving each one a token smile.

Dictation 7

The opening moment of the program was very boring, a token of what was to follow. With a stony poker face, Ann slipped out quietly and went to the ball game.

Dictation 8

Jim went poking around in the dump, hoping to locate old bottles. In a pile of clothing he found some broken glass. It focused the sunlight on some paper that began to smoke. He stamped out the fire.

Dictation 9

Dawn was jabbing the open fire with a poker. A spark flew out and for a moment she couldn't locate it. Then she smelled something burning. It made a hole in the rug.

Dictation 10

It was a bad moment when they could not locate the boy with the broken leg. Then they got his dog. Not a word was spoken while the dog went poking around and sniffing. Suddenly with a sharp bark he ran to a tree where the boy lay.

Dictation 11

The boys were going to play poker on a broken table in the old shack. Sam gave a bogus check and they opened up on him. He pretended to be joking, but he got a stony look.

Dictation 12

They were playing poker and Dan lost some cash to Bud. He gave Bud a bogus check. When Bud found that out he went to Dan with a stony look and opened up a fight. A lot of things got broken.

Dictation 13

The thing lay out in the open on the stony ground. It was a broken wheel of a bike. Poking at it, June said jokingly that the rider could not have gone far. Going on down the hill, she was astonished to find a boy and the front part of the bike.

Ū

Dictation 1

The heat was brutal and the humidity was high. It was inhuman to expect students to study. They united in saying no.

Dictation 2

June was playing music. She dropped the needle and ruined the platter. She felt stupid. Well, we are all human.

Dictation 3

I was not stupid, only human. I put so much fuel on the fire that it began to burn the wall. I saw my duty. I called, and the fire department sent a unit to put it out.

Dictation 4

There was a furious storm over Utah. Fuel ran low and houses were ruined. Human misery was high. The situation was worse than usual.

Dictation 5

It was a brutal day, hot, humid and muggy. The sky grew dark and a squall passed over the city. The fury of the storm was highly unusual. It ruined a lot of trees.

Dictation 6

At camp it was Beth's duty to blow the bugle in the morning to get everybody up. She stupidly overslept. Slipping on her Bermuda shorts, she dashed out and blew taps. The camp leader was furious. After all, Beth was only human.

Three Lists

CHAPTER 17

Nothing is needed in the Teacher's Manual to accompany **Chapter 17.**

More Phonograms

CHAPTER 18

IE

Friend is more easily taught as a learned word.

EW

Grow, grew, etc. shows a pattern that may help to clarify the confusion of **threw** and **through,** of **know, no** and **now.**

IE as /ē/

Dictation 1

The chief looked splendid. His shield was shiny and his look was fierce. After a brief run, he stopped the thief.

Dictation 2

The thief dashed out of the bank. The fiend sprinted across the field to shield himself in the bushes by the pier. The police chief sped to the place and the thief yielded to the law.

Dictation 3

The chief had a fine silver badge. She looked at the cars stopping at the red light. The thief slipped out of the bank behind her back and mingled with the passersby. The chief saw nothing.

Dictation 4

The thief grabbed my niece's handbag and started running. He stubbed his toe on a bulging root and came to grief. As he fell, I jumped on him and gave him a piece of my mind.

Dictation 5

Meg shielded her face from the sun. She was looking across the field for her puppy. She had left the gate open for a brief moment and her new retriever had run off. She called and called and at last the dog yielded to her voice and came back. It was a big relief.

Dictation 6

Ann saw the thief go out of the window and run across the field. She gave a shriek and dashed to the church. The priest phoned the police. To her relief they came promptly. She believed the robber was shielding herself in the woods.

EW

Dictation 1

The winning crew flew a flag. The wind blew it. As they landed, they drew cheers and shouts. Everyone threw them kisses.

Dictation 2

Rose was in a stew. She had a new shirt on. Someone was screwy and threw paint around. Rose flew off to avoid getting spattered.

Dictation 3

Jack tried to brew some beer. It blew up. His boss grew very angry and nearly threw him out. No wonder. It was a screwy thing to do.

Dictation 4

My nephew sat on the dock and drew the ships. The wind blew his paper away, and he grew upset. A boat crew stopped chewing gum and flew to my nephew's resue. They got his picture back.

Dictation 5

Jack knew how to make a good stew. He threw some beef into a heavy pot, added spices and red wine, and simmered slowly. It grew so tender that it hardly needed chewing. The smell drew the crew to it before it was ready.

EIGH as /ā/

Dictation 1

My neighbor went with me to the freight station. We saw eighty-cars. We also picked up a package that weighed a lot.

Dictation 2

April had a fat neighbor weighing two hundred and eighty pounds. She believed that her neighbor ate all day. It must be hard, carrying all that freight around.

UE

Dictation 1

It is true that the value of a dime has shrunk. It made me blue to think of all the bills that were due.

Dictation 2

It was a blue stamp, torn and shabby. Tom glued it onto the envelope and restored its value.

Dictation 3

"I have broken your statue. What is its true value?" asked Frank.
"I have no clue," said Jack.
"Well, don't sue me. I will glue it together."

Dictation 4

The sky was blue and the day was bright and sunny. Frank argued that they take a hike. The girl did not value hiking. True to her nature, she insisted on riding.

Words Ending in EY

The monkey went down the chimney into the galley and stole the money. He took it out and shared it with the donkey. He wouldn't give any to the turkeys, for he was angry with them.

Exercise 5 — page 123

Be sure the students can read these words. If you want them to be able to spell one that might be useful to them, such as **money** or **key,** put it on the list of learned words.

Problems

You will probably need the sections **And, a, an; Its, it's;** and **Go, Do,** and perhaps **AUGH** and **OUGH.** The rest of this chapter is a matter of the teacher's choice. You may want to use it for variety, or to refer to it if a question comes up.

AUGH

Dictation 1

Robin had taught herself to wake up at any time. She caught her plane because she got up in plenty of time.

Dictation 2

Frank taught his dog to catch a ball. He caught it in his jaws. His daughter grabbed the ball. He did not think she was naughty. She was playing a game.

Dictation 3

The pitcher threw the ball and the catcher caught it. A naughty puppy got in the way and the catcher dropped it. The runners took another base. The umpire yelled at the dog and hopefully taught it a lesson.

Dictation 4

Linda taught the monster some tricks. He was not a naughty monster, only a sad one. He would not slaughter a fly. He caught her ideas in a flash and was delighted to have some fun.

Dictation 5

Martha took a long walk along the shore. A squall came up quickly. It caught her by surprise far from home. A cold wind blew and the sky grew dark. Then the rain drenched her. It taught her to be more careful.

Go, Do

Dictation 1

Does she like swimming? She goes to the shore every day and has done so for a long time, even when summer has gone.

Dictation 2

Before Tom goes to work in the morning, he makes his bed. He doesn't mind. He has done it all his life.

Dictation 3

When Bob has gone to work, his son goes at the kitchen with a will. He does not like it to be dirty. When it is done, he goes shopping.

Dictation 4

"Does this street go north?"
"I don't know. I haven't gone this way. I think it goes by the station."

Dictation 5

Frank goes along with the rules. He has always done so. He doesn't think it right to break them. Things have gone well with him.

Dictation 6

When Mary doesn't like something, she goes into a rage. She hasn't done so this week, but she probably will. She has sometimes gone into quite a fit when she feels obstructed.

Dictation 7

"Where is Pete?"
"He has gone to the airport."
"Has he done his report?"
"No. You know Peter. He goes his own way. He doesn't like to do reports."
"Well, who does?"

Dictation 8

"I should like to go with her."
"Too bad, she has already gone. I would have stopped her if I could."
"Never mind. I have a good many things to do."
"Right. You haven't done any picking up yet. Whose toys are those?"

OUGH

Dictation 1

Pat brought her checkbook and bought an old car. She thought it was fine. He ought to have been more careful, because it soon broke down.

Dictation 2

Jack saw a handsome jacket. He fought temptation. Then he gave in and bought it. He brought it home to show his girl.

Dictation 3

I bought a ticket for the sweepstakes. I fought my way to the booth to get it and brought it happily home. I thought the drawing would be in the paper and sought my name in it. It was there. What a wonder, I had won.

Dictation 4

Jill ought to have bought the land a long time ago. Now it was very costly. She sought a solution to the problem and thought she had found one. She brought her maps farther north and hunted for a likely spot.

Dictation 5

Helen bought a new ribbon for her hair. It was charming, but a very odd shade. Then she sought a dress to go with it. She ought to have done it the other way around. She thought she would go to a sale and fought her way through the crowd. She brought home two dresses which did not match the ribbon at all.

<h2 style="text-align:center">ACE</h2>

Dictation 1

The race took place on April 19. The strain of the city hills showed in their faces. The runner from Denmark was first. She took her win gracefully.

Dictation 2

Let's face it. The pace of the rat race is getting faster and faster. There is little trace of grace left in life. We must find a small space to relax.

Dictation 3

Any way you slice it, the space race is over for the time being. Our aces had a grand lift-off from the moon without a trace of hardship.

<h2 style="text-align:center">ICE</h2>

Dictation 1

It was a very nice wedding. The bride and groom were pelted with rice. Everyone was given a slice of cake. In a trice it was all over.

Dictation 2

For dinner we will have chicken and rice and then that spicy cake with the icing on it. Paul said it was nice and twice cut himself a slice.

<h2 style="text-align:center">ANCE</h2>

Riding along on his bike, Tommy fell into a trance. He was having a fancy dream about being the star of a football game. Bumping into a fence, he hit his head and went home crying. His father did not mince matters while sticking on a plaster. He called him a dunce.

<h2 style="text-align:center">AIN</h2>

Dictation 1

The captain took his friend to see the fountain. Against the backdrop of the mountains it was a grand sight. He tossed in a coin for good luck.

Dictation 2

There was certainly something wrong with the plane. It was bumping up and down with the changing air drafts. The wind was the villain. Then the plane slipped sideways and almost crashed against the mountain.

More About the Doubling Rule

CHAPTER 20

Exercise 1 — page 129

admitting	forgotten
preferred	beginning
equipping	propeller

Exercise 2 — page 130

transmitted	referred	numbering	profitable
gardening	forbidden	permitted	unforgettable

Exercise 3 — page 130

performance	invented	suffered	deferring
entered	compelling	deferment	piloting
regretting	contended		

Dictation 1

Jane took her fishing equipment to the shore, but there was no admittance. She had forgotten that fishing was forbidden in that lake. She found the fact regrettable.

Dictation 2

The puppy was forbidden to get on the bed. Whenever Eve saw him she compelled him to get off. As soon as she left the bedroom he got back on. This was a regrettable trick. She had forgotten how uncontrolled he was.

Dictation 3

James was planning to go hunting. He had excellent equipment. He looked around to see whether he had forgotten anything. That might be regrettable. Then he propelled his little car down the road.

Dictation 4

She had remarkable hi-fi equipment. Her bedroom was equipped with racks containing her records. She had allotted space for every part. It was regrettable that the sound was so loud.

Dictation 5

Amy admitted that she did not like fish. She preferred steak. Someone offered her whale steak but she referred to it as stinking. She ate chowder willingly and numbered lobster among her delights.

Dictation 6

Sam and his friend went to the baseball game. They were beginning to get very hot. When the game was over, he conferred with her on this subject. He did not want her suffering. Then he propelled her into a diner and ordered iced tea.

Dictation 7

I put the container with my equipment into the car. Gathering up my papers, I looked around to see whether I had forgotten anything. Then I dashed off. It was a gripping performance.

Dictation 8

The forbidden transmitter was hidden in a hole. With it Jim was equipped to send messages in secret. If he got stopped, it might be regrettable. He might become the forgotten man.

Dictation 9

Val was committed to a speaking engagement. She admitted to herself that she was frightened but she felt compelled to do her best. She acquitted herself very well. Her performance was splendid.

Dictation 10

Market gardening is a perishable business, depending on the weather. Appearance must be excellent. The farmer must be equipped for every mishap. Containers must be appealing. But for a careful person, it can be a profitable commitment.

Dictation 11

The grass was glittering with frost and shining in the early sunny morning. We started slipping and sliding on it. We had forgotten what fun it was. No equipment was needed. In hiking you were bogged down with a knapsack. In golf you dragged around a bag containing clubs. In fishing you were committed to rod, reel and tackle box. But for this sport you were already equipped with shoes. And we slipped, skidded and skated some more.

Dictation 12

In the gathering darkness Ann gained admittance and went to her allotted seat. She found the performance excellent but the play regrettably dull. She had a commitment to her newspaper and before the last appearance of the star she propelled herself through the crowd. As befitted a good critic, she transmitted her thoughts to the typewriter in clear English and had forgotten the play by the time they were printed.